FACETS OF INDIAN POVERTY

About the Authors

K. L. Datta is an officer of the Indian Economic Service, 1975 Batch. Graduated in Economics (Hons.) from Calcutta University, M.A. (Economics) from Calcutta University and Manchester University. He has been posted in different capacities in the Planning Commission, 1977-85 and as Deputy Secretary in the Ministry of Finance, 1988-93. Presently posted as Joint Adviser (Perspective Planning) in the Planning Commission.

Savita Sharma is an officer of the Indian Statistical Service, 1980 Batch. Graduated in Mathematics (Hons.) from Delhi University, M.Sc and Ph.D in Agricultural Statistics from Indian Agricultural Research Institute, New Delhi. She has been posted in different capacities in the Planning Commission since 1983 and presently is Director in the Planning Commission.

FACETS OF INDIAN POVERTY

K.L. DATTA
SAVITA SHARMA

CONCEPT PUBLISHING COMPANY, NEW DELHI - 110059

ISBN 81-7022-959-6 (PB)

First Published 2002

Published and Printed by

Ashok Kumar Mittal
Concept Publishing Company
A/15-16, Commercial Block, Mohan Garden
NEW DELHI -110059 (India)

Phones : 5648039, 5649024
Fax : 091-11-5648053
Email : *publishing@conceptpub.com*

Montek S. Ahluwalia
Member
Planning Commission

सदस्य
योजना आयोग
योजना भवन
नई दिल्ली-११०००१.
Yojana Bhavan
New Delhi-110 001.
Tel.:91-11-3719218
Fax:91-11-3719593

FOREWORD

The measurement of poverty in India has been a subject of active interest and discussion in the academic community and also in the Press ever since a Planning Commission Working Group set out a minimum requirement in 1962. A great deal of research has gone into refining the concepts and quantifying the minimum consumption requirement, which form the basis of the poverty line. There has also been a lively debate associated with efforts to measure the number and percentage of people living below the poverty line and especially to assess time trends in poverty.

The sixties and seventies produced a substantial body of literature on estimating poverty in India and trends revealed by these estimates were used to assess the impact of Government plans and programmes on the level of poverty. Poverty estimates assumed added importance in the early eighties when the Planning Commission began to make official estimates of poverty at national and state level and to use these estimates in the allocation of Government funds in income redistributive schemes.

There can be little doubt that reduction of poverty must be the litmus test for gauging the success of India's planning and development strategy. This book is the result of detailed research on the theoretical and empirical aspects of the various facets of poverty in India by two officers of the Planning Commission writing in their personal capacity. It contains certain hitherto unexplored areas in the measurement of poverty and presents solid facts about poverty and deprivation, which can add real substance to the on-going poverty debate. It provides sub-state level estimates of consumption and the inequality in its distribution across different income classes of the population, which are rare. The estimates of poverty by occupation, socio-economic groups, gender and religion of the population can form useful inputs for locating the vulnerable groups.

The analysis of poverty ratio has been backed up by distributional indices of poverty with a forceful plea to replace the Share of Poor (SP) estimated from the Poverty Ratio (PR) by the measure of Contribution to Total Poverty (CTP) estimated from the Squared Poverty Gap (SPG) in the matter of allocation of funds under poverty alleviation programmes. This is only one of the many interesting new insights contained in this book.

Poverty is a multi-dimensional concept, and perception about how best to measure it will necessarily evolve over time. The discussion on the indices of poverty, including various distributional indices in this book will be handy reference for all those interested in the subject. I believe that this book forms a substantial contribution to the body of knowledge on poverty in its various dimensions.

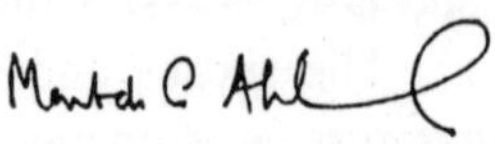

(Montek Singh Ahluwalia)

PREFACE

Reduction in poverty and inequality, and improvement in levels of living have been among the central objectives of Indian planning during the past half a century. An assessment of the indicators that describe the levels of living and dictate the state of poverty becomes necessary not only for having an idea about the present state of affairs but also for formulating future policies, and to make developmental planning more effective. The question precisely is: what are these indicators and how these can be quantified – an aspect that has challenged planners and policy makers not only in India and similar low income developing countries, but also in the developed world.

The issue thus relates to the choice of variables that can stand as fair measures of the prevalence of poverty. Intuitively it may be felt that since poor people have less income, the average level of income would decide the state of poverty. However, income has rarely been used to measure poverty in low income developing countries, where a large proportion of the population depend on agriculture for their livelihood and derive a major portion of income in kind. Consumer expenditure data have been found to be more appropriate for analysis of levels of living and poverty in developing countries precisely for the reason that it reflects more accurately the people's actual level of well-being, while income data are more concerned with people's potential level of living. Income in kind, such as consumption of own produce, is often valued at producer's prices, that is, the price received by the producer at the point of sale, which results in underestimation of people's actual level of living. The reason is that if the person had not produced the good himself, he would have to buy it from the market at the consumer's price, which always exceeds the producer's price because of transport and trade margins.

The issue of sidetracking income also lies in the complexity of its computation. In countries where a substantial portion of economic transactions are non-monetised, accurate assessment of income becomes problematic. In addition, people are frequently unwilling to reveal their true levels of income for a variety of reasons. Studies by the World Bank (Shaohua Chen and Martin Ravallion, for example) have also confirmed the use of consumption data as an indicator of well-being for reasons of reliability apart from the fact that it captures the long run welfare levels better than current income. Thus, consumption data can be obtained more accurately than income data from nationwide surveys conducted by the statistical agencies of a country.

When poverty is viewed as a lack of income or consumption, merely assessing the average levels is not sufficient. The class distribution of income/consumption is also an essential element in determining poverty. It is for this reason that regionally the relation between per capita consumption and poverty has not been found to be uniform in India. The relation is also not uniform between inequality and poverty. Both these factors have to be taken into account simultaneously while assessing poverty.

India, long stratified by the labyrinth of religion and caste, finds inequality in distribution of per capita consumption within a particular region often being masked by severe inequality in its distribution between sociological and occupational categories. Within a region, between-category inequality is so pronounced that makes it necessary to assess consumption and poverty by a cross classification of occupation, socio-economic and gender groups.

Inequality in India, as measured by the Lorenz ratio of per capita consumption distribution, has remained nearly stable during the last thirty years or so and a large part of the decline in poverty has come from the growth in incomes. Simulation exercises reveal that high growth rate with modest decline in inequality can significantly increase the income and consumption of the poor and thereby reduce poverty. But the critical issue is how to raise consumption with equity, that is, to generate a growth path which is more equitable and benefits the poor most. Though there are studies associated with the idea that faster agricultural growth is poverty reducing, the course is really not well-defined and experiences under similar conditions vary.

The inter-temporal changes in poverty have not been uniform across regions and sociological and occupational categories. Similar change in per capita consumption and inequality has produced diverse results across regions and categories. Agricultural growth has not been uniform across the country and hence it is not expected to produce a uniform impact on alleviation of poverty. High income growth has reduced poverty only in some regions. There are states where poverty could be reduced even with low income through the state-sponsored food subsidy schemes which besides raising the level of food consumption kept the food prices, and in turn, the general price level low. These experiences perhaps call for a differentiated approach to the problem of poverty rather than a single unified command across the length and breadth of the country. In fact, effective poverty alleviation measures would require identification of poor by regions and categories and prescriptions for poverty reduction would vary in tune with the characteristics of the population.

Poverty analysis in India generally has four dimensions. These are: (a) definition of poverty, (b) measurement of poverty, (c) identification of the poor and (d) design and implementation of poverty alleviation programmes.

Not many studies have been made about the definition of poverty and fixation of poverty line in case of India. There are only two, and both of them have come from the Indian Planning Commission. The first in 1962 was prepared by a Working Group and the other in 1979 by a Task Force. Studies on Indian poverty in the sixties and seventies were based on the 1962 Working Group poverty line of the Planning Commission. Most of these studies were crafted onto the level of living by decomposing this national level poverty line into state-specific poverty lines using a variety of deflators. Since the eighties, poverty estimation was being made from the 1979 Task Force poverty lines, which were also at national level, but separated into rural and urban areas. Although the Planning Commission appointed an Expert Group in 1989 to go into the question of re-defining the poverty line, it did not find enough justification to change the same. The Expert Group accepted the national level poverty lines set by the Task Force and disaggregated them into state-specific poverty lines using state-specific consumer price indices and inter-state price differentials.

The issue of measurement of poverty has attracted considerable attention of researchers and policy makers in India and the ensuing debate has been vigorous and illuminating. A precise estimate of poverty by region and socio-economic categories is necessary for its use as parameters in the mathematical models used in plan formulation. Indeed, it is a complex task. The poor in India will be amused by the relentless pursuit of researchers to find their exact number.

The identification of poor by area, region, occupation and social categories becomes necessary for implementation of poverty alleviation programmes. The identification is being done in India on a census basis at an interval of around five years, normally at the beginning of a five year plan period. The census, at present, is conducted in two stages. First, on the basis of certain exclusion criteria, such as, threshold level of income and ownership of land, building, consumer durables and agricultural implements, some families are declared as non-poor. In the second stage, the total consumption, both purchased from the market and home grown, are gathered from the remaining families. This total consumption of the family is divided by its total number of persons in order to obtain the per capita consumption. If this per capita consumption of the family falls below the poverty line, it is identified as poor.

The poverty alleviation programmes, conceived as a part of the income redistributive schemes and framed for direct income generation of the poor, bypassing the general growth process are of two types. These are : (a) asset generation programme and (b) employment generation programme. The asset generation programmes are designed for those poor having requisite skills so that public assistance combined with private entrepreneurship and skill produces a regular flow of income which, when added to the income originating from the general growth process, allows the beneficiary to cross the poverty line. The employment generation programmes are generally offered to those poor who have nothing but their raw labour power to sell. The latter programmes do not allow the beneficiary to cross the poverty line permanently. In the absence of employment provided by such programmes, the beneficiary may rejoin the poor group.

Although a remarkable amount of sophistication is shown in the use of data (e.g., consumption, prices, nutrition, etc.) for estimation of poverty ratio, it needs be emphasized that the poverty ratio, which is the ratio of number of poor to total population, is unable to capture the depth and severity of poverty in an adequate manner mainly because it makes no distinction within the broad category of the poor depending upon their actual level of consumption and deprivation. Poverty Gap Ratio (PGR), which adjusts the poverty ratio with the difference between the per capita consumption of the poor and the poverty line, expressed as a percentage of the poverty line, is a measure that captures the depth of poverty and indicates the magnitude of the effort required to shift the consumption of all persons below the poverty line to the level of the poverty line. The severity of poverty is captured from the Squared Poverty Gap (SPG), which is composed of the poverty ratio, poverty gap ratio and the consumption distribution of the poor. This measure explicitly takes into account the higher intensity of efforts required to address the people who are progressively further below the poverty line in order to bring them out of poverty.

The indices of depth and severity of poverty mentioned above should replace the poverty ratio, which is also known as head-count ratio. The distributional indices should be computed at the disaggregated level of region and socio-economic categories to identify the poor and allocation of funds under poverty alleviation programmes made accordingly. This will make the identification process more effective and the allocation of funds more efficient.

Growth and equity, for their direct association with poverty, occupy an important place in the planning process of India and have been given rigorous treatment in planning exercises. The set of issues at the moment center around the relation between growth, equity and poverty and, in particular, how growth and equity impact upon the incidence of poverty. Alongside, another set of issues relate to disparity in urban-rural poverty and poverty by regions, occupation and socio-economic groups, gender, religion, family size and land possession. Answers to these questions, which have been attempted during the past five decades in successive five year plans in some way or other, form the central theme of this study. It has been structured with the planner's view of poverty, its conceptualization, quantification and the measures for amelioration in the successive five year plans. In the process, it goes on to document systematically the various facets of poverty, by region and occupation and sociological categories as well as the major issues in the measurement of poverty line and poverty in the Indian context.

These features of Indian poverty are segmented into seven chapters. The first chapter traces the manner and method of conceptualization of poverty in India. The second chapter deals with the inter-temporal movement of various poverty indices. Chapter three assesses consumption and poverty by occupation and socio-economic groups and by gender and religion of the population. It assesses the impact of land possession and household size on poverty. The assessment is also made by cross-classifying occupation and socio-economic groups.

In India, although the district is treated as the focal point of administration, the disaggregated estimates of poverty are available only at the state level. Regional level estimates of poverty are not available and those of indicators of levels of living are rare. In order to fill this gap, Chapter four makes an estimate of consumption and inequality at sub-state level and assesses their features. The sub-state level estimates relate to NSS (National Sample Survey) regions, which are formed by grouping contiguous districts having similarity in respect of density of population and cropping pattern. Chapter five deals with the poverty at regional level. The poor are further divided into groups, such as, very poor and moderately poor, and the non-poor as lower and upper non-poor. The relationship between consumption, inequality and poverty is traced in: (a) regions with high and low poverty, (b) regions with high and low consumption and (c) regions with high and low inequality. It also traces the concentration of population and poor in specific regions.

Chapter six deals with the estimation of depth and severity of poverty and emphasises the need for using distributional indices in the measurement of poverty and in the allocation of funds under anti-poverty programmes. Poverty Gap Ratio and Squared Poverty

Gap are assessed at sub-state (NSS region) level and it is argued that Contribution to Total Poverty (CTP) computed from Squared Poverty Gap should be used to allocate funds for poverty alleviation programmes in place of the Share of Poor estimated from the Poverty Ratio. In order to locate the target groups, the CTPs are estimated for occupation, socio-economic groups and for gender and religion of the population. Finally, Chapter seven assesses the robustness of the poverty estimates utilizing the calorie intake and per capita consumption for different sections of the population and lists the emerging issues in the estimation of poverty in recent days.

To conclude, as a result of planned economic development during the past half a century, there has been a near trebling of per capita real income and more than doubling of per capita real consumption in India. This increase in income and consumption has reduced the level and intensity of poverty. Using a fixed poverty line, the decline in the number of poor and consequent improvement in the level of living of the people across the length and breadth of the country is not denied. However, the objective of reducing poverty and improving the levels of living of the population also requires attention to the criteria that go beyond income and consumption. Socio-economic indicators such as life expectancy, literacy, etc. are as important to quality of life as income or consumption. For instance, there are regions with high income and low poverty and yet with a low level of socio-economic indicators. Further, high infant mortality rate is witnessed in some of India's most prosperous regions. This paradoxical situation is often lost sight of. Therefore, great care needs to be exercised in interpreting poverty estimates, particularly when inter-regional or inter-country comparisons are being made. Although, income or consumption based poverty measures are certainly indicative of levels of well-being, no definitive conclusions can be drawn without reference to other socio-economic indicators which capture the non-material aspects of living.

K.L. DATTA

SAVITA SHARMA

ACKNOWLEDGEMENTS

Many people have helped in finalizing this study by way of intellectual, academic and moral support. It is not possible to mention each one of them here. Dr. Pronab Sen, Adviser, Planning Commission needs special mention. Without his encouragement and unflinching support, it would have been nearly impossible to complete the study. This book has a heavy programming responsibility. The computer softwares used in this exercise have been developed by Shri R.K. Pruthi, Senior Technical Director, National Informatics Centre. No word is sufficient for this strenuous job shouldered by him. The assistance of Shri S.V. Ramana Murthy, Senior Research Officer is gratefully acknowledged and of Shri Sanjay Gupta, Computer Grade-I, who has smilingly typed numerous drafts of the tables that finally appear in this book. Ms. Amrita Datta has assisted in the preparation of the index.

K.L. DATTA

SAVITA SHARMA

CONTENTS

LIST OF TABLES

TABLES IN TEXT

1

THE PLANNING PROCESS AND POVERTY

The planning process in India displays a remarkable stability in its objectives, which can be summed up as growth, equity, modernisation and self-reliance. In these, poverty alleviation has been at the centre-stage of the development strategy.

In the initial years, a distinction between poor and non-poor was not as much necessary because of the low level of development. The economy was stagnant; per capita income was abysmally low and its distribution was highly unequal. The prime need, at that stage, was to build the necessary infrastructure to generate sufficient income. The first two Five Year Plans (1951-56, 1956-61) concentrated mainly on this theme, though the mathematical structure of the Second Five Year Plan (Mahalanobis model) attached adequate importance to labour-intensive techniques of production and production of wage goods so that the benefits of growth could reach a larger section of the population, while building up the necessary base for agricultural and industrial infrastructure. As the economy grew at a rate of 4% per year in the first ten years (1951-61) talks about poverty and a proportionately greater benefit to the poor gained ground by allowing them a larger share of income through a more equitable distribution of the fruits of growth. This necessitated a decision on the minimum requirement for healthy living.

A Working Group of the Planning Commission quantified the minimum (food and non-food) requirement of the individuals for a healthy living in 1962. The money value of the minimum requirement, known as the poverty line, was set as per capita consumption expenditure of Rs.20 per month at 1960-61 prices. Most of the studies on Indian poverty in the late 1960s and early 1970s were crafted on to the level of living by decomposing this national poverty line into first, rural and urban, and then to state-specific poverty lines using a variety of deflators (rather inflators, as economists have always used this term). These studies primarily focussed on whether or not agricultural performance had anything to do with rural poverty. It was a crude measure of poverty, no doubt, and marginal change in the poverty ratio often forced diverse conclusions. Yet, no one can deny that a remarkable amount of sophistication in correcting consumption data, calculating class-specific deflators, etc., accompany these estimates of poverty, which were essentially the work of P. D. Ojha, V. M. Dandekar, Nilkantha Rath, Amartya K. Sen, Pranab K. Bardhan, Ashok Rudra, B.S. Minhas, I. Z. Bhatty, T. N. Srinivasan, Montek Singh Ahluwalia, and many others.

In the late 1960s, two programmes, viz., Small Farmers' Development Agency (SFDA) and Marginal Farmers and Agricultural Labourers (MFAL), were incorporated into agricultural planning. The main plank of these two programmes was special incentive to the poorest of the poor in agriculture, for raising their incomes, and can be termed as the first step towards the formulation of direct anti-poverty programmes.

The growth strategy in the Fifth Five Year Plan (1974-79) contained certain programmes of social consumption code named Minimum Needs Programme. This programme was in the areas of health, water supply, rural roads, sanitation, medical facilities and nutrition in rural areas. This was not an income generation programme, but certainly had a content of benefit towards the poor and lower middle class by way of dissemination of the growth impulses.

The Fifth Five Year Plan assessed the consumption demand of the bottom 30% of the population through a consumption sub-model. This sub-model was integrated with the Fifth Plan model, which in turn, was an integration of the Leontief Input-Output

System with the models of macro-economic growth belonging to the family of Harrod-Domar. This mathematical quantification of the consumption demand of the poorer section of the population (bottom 30%) and its integration with the overall rate of growth of the economy, ensuring appropriate inter-sectoral consistency, opened varied treatment of the concept of poverty into the planning exercises. This piece of theoretical work done by Prof. Sukhamoy Chakravarty changed the language and approach of Indian Planning.

The late 1970s and early 1980s witnessed a sea change in the strategy for poverty alleviation. From the Sixth Five Year Plan (1980-85), the strategy was settled as "growth with redistribution", which means that along with the general growth process, special schemes are to be formulated for direct income generation of the poor, to achieve a faster reduction in poverty. This necessitated the formulation of a well-defined index of poverty and location of the poor by their residence and occupation. The Planning Commission, in the Sixth Plan, constituted a "Task Force on Projection of Minimum Needs and Effective Consumption Demand" with the objective of constructing such an index and the method of determining the consumption demand of the poor and non-poor. The Task Force estimated the minimum requirement of the individuals separately in rural and urban areas because of the distinct composition of the two regions in terms of income generation and occupation. It worked out the average calorie requirement of the population by their place of residence and the consumption expenditure necessary to meet the calorie requirement, which is widely known as the poverty line.

The strategy of growth with redistribution gave birth to income redistributive and employment generation schemes. Allocation of funds under such schemes, first at national level and then distribution of the national corpus among the States/Union Territories began to be determined on the basis of poverty estimates made by the Planning Commission using the Task Force method. But, the poverty estimates itself came under attack, mostly from the state governments. This requires a brief digression into the method of estimation of poverty by Task Force.

Task Force

The Task Force, under the Chairmanship of Dr. Y.K. Alagh, clearly recognised that the poverty line would have to take into account the fact that minimum consumption requirement would vary between different categories of persons depending upon their age, sex and the nature of work performed. Since the poverty line is a summary measure encapsulating all these differences, it would need to be a weighted average of the normative consumption needs of each of these categories. The Task Force used the age-sex-activity distribution of the population and the calorie norms of Indian Council of Medical Research (ICMR) to work out the per capita daily calorie requirements as 2435 kcal in rural areas and 2095 kcal in urban areas. In view of the importance of the poverty line and the debate surrounding it, the population weighting diagram and the calorie norms are given below.

Average Calorie Requirment

Age-Sex-Activity Group	Weighting Diagram:Rural	Weighting Diagram:Urban	Calorie Norm
1. Children			
a. Less than 1 year	2.72	2.49	650
b. 1 to 4 years	8.21	7.66	1200
c. 4 to 7 years	7.99	7.53	1500
d. 7 to 10 years	7.47	7.66	1800
e. 10 to 13 years	7.46	7.66	2100
2. Adolescents:13 to 15 years			
a. Boys	2.37	2.36	2500
b. Girls	2.22	2.23	2200
3. 15 years and Above			
I. Workers:Male			
a. Heavy	22.63	3.83	3900
b. Moderate	2.13	7.72	2800
c. Sedentary	2.66	14.10	2400
II. Workers:Female			
a. Heavy	10.88	1.47	3000
b. Moderate	0.93	1.40	2200
c. Sedentary	0.59	2.87	1900
III. Non-Workers			
a. Male	3.92	8.62	2400
b. Female	17.82	22.40	1900
4. Average Calorie Norm	2431.91	2093.71	

The population weighting diagram is based on (a) the projected age-sex structure of the population for 1982-83 (III Projection) of the Expert Committee on Population (1977), (b) 1971 census occupational structure, and (c) usual status participation rates from NSS employment data of 1972-73 (NSS, 27th Round). The population weighting diagram coupled with the calorie norms yielded the average requirement as 2432 kcal per day in rural areas and 2094 kcal per day in urban areas. Adding the extra calorie needs of pregnant and lactating women, the daily requirement came to be 2436 kcal in rural areas and 2097 kcal in urban areas. These were rounded off to 2435 kcal in rural areas and 2095 kcal in urban areas and the per capita consumption expenditure required to attain these calorie norms (i.e., the poverty line) were worked out from the NSS consumption expenditure data (1973-74, NSS 28th Round) as Rs. 49.09 per month in rural areas and Rs. 56.64 per month in urban areas. These poverty lines thus, conform to a consumption basket that satisfies the above calorie norm and meets a minimum of non-food requirements, such as clothing, shelter, transport, etc. For the sake of simplicity, these norms were further rounded-off to 2400 kcal in rural areas and 2100 kcal in urban areas.

The percentage of people below the poverty line (poverty ratio) are estimated from the expenditure class-wise distribution of persons obtained from consumer expenditure surveys of the National Sample Survey (NSS) Organisation. This distribution of persons is not used directly as the consumption estimated in National Accounts Statistics (NAS) of Central Statistical Organisation (CSO) differs from that of NSS. In the absence of requisite data, the NSS consumption was adjusted to the level of CSO consumption, *pro-rata*, among different expenditure groups of the population. To estimate poverty for the subsequent years, the poverty line of 1973-74 was updated initially by the Wholesale Price Index (WPI), then by the private consumption deflator of the CSO.

The Task Force did not outline a methodology to estimate state-wise poverty. Its methodology at the national level was simply extended to states by (a) applying the national poverty line uniformly to all the states, and (b) adjusting state level NSS consumption distribution *pro-rata* to CSO consumption.

The application of national poverty line uniformly to all the states to derive state-wise poverty was questioned because of differential rates of inflation among the states. In tandem, the *pro-rata* adjustment of NSS consumption to CSO level of consumption, first in rural and urban areas and then within each area, for different expenditure groups of the population created increasing concern with time in view of the inverse relationship between the extent of this discrepancy and the poverty ratio. When the Task Force recommended such a method of adjustment in the late 1970s, the discrepancy between the two was less than 5%. It increased steadily to 39% in 1993-94, which changed to 61% with change in the base year of calculation of CSO consumption from 1980-81 to 1993-94. The poverty ratio reduced as a result of this adjustment; but the relative position of the states remained almost unchanged. This happened at a time when the poverty ratio was increasingly being applied in the allocation of central assistance to states not only under various anti-poverty programmes but also under several developmental or social security programmes. A reduced number of poor means a lower allocation and that prompted the states to voice their anxiety over the Task Force method.

In brief, the Task Force method appeared inadequate in giving a representative picture of poverty in India for the following reasons.

(a) The adjustment procedure, whereby the discrepancy between the CSO and the NSS estimates of consumption was allocated on a *pro-rata* basis across all expenditure classes. The general feeling was that the discrepancy should not have been so high for the lower expenditure classes.

(b) The application of a single poverty line each for rural and urban areas for all the states, which implicitly assumes absence of price differential across the states.

(c) The assumption of a fixed consumption basket of the poor overtime.

(d) The assumption of uniform consumption basket for all the states.

(e) The choice of deflators to represent price changes in the poverty line.

Expert Group

The Planning Commission acted by constituting an Expert Group on Estimation of Proportion and Number of Poor in September 1989. The job earmarked was: "to look into the methodology for estimation of poverty at national and state level and also to go into the question of re-defining the poverty line, if necessary." The Expert Group recommended that the Task Force national level poverty lines, which are per capita monthly consumption expenditure of Rs. 49.09 in rural areas and Rs. 56.64 in urban areas, anchored in the per capita daily intake of 2400 kcal in rural areas and 2100 kcal in urban areas with reference to the consumption pattern as obtained in 1973-74, be adopted as the base line, and that these norms be adopted uniformly for all the states. The Expert Group disaggregated these national level poverty lines into state-specific poverty lines on the basis of state-specific prices and inter-state price differential. Using these state-specific poverty lines, the poverty ratios are estimated from the state-specific consumption distribution of the NSS, directly, i.e., without any adjustment to CSO consumption.

The Expert Group method, thus captures the cost of living in each state more accurately through the state-specific poverty lines, though it is the national consumption basket, which is evaluated at the state's prices. In the absence of adjustment of NSS consumption expenditure data, the characteristics of the distribution remain intact. However, it is often forgotten that estimate of poverty made from NSS consumption expenditure data alone means an automatic adjustment of the consumption of the non-poor group, by allocating them the entire difference.

2

THE INDICES OF POVERTY

The Planning Commission is the nodal agency in the Government of India for estimation of poverty. It estimates the incidence of poverty at the national and state level using the Expert Group method. Following this method, poverty at the national level is estimated as weighted average of state-wise poverty. State-wise poverty is estimated from state-specific poverty lines and consumer expenditure distribution of states obtained from the large sample surveys conducted by the National Sample Survey Organisation at an interval of approximately five years.

Poverty Line

The Expert Group disaggregated the national rural and urban poverty lines of 1973-74 estimated by the Task Force into state-specific poverty lines using state-specific price indices and inter-state price differential. The state-wise poverty lines, thus represent the amount of consumption expenditure necessary in the state, at the state's prices, in order to acquire the national consumption basket. The state-specific poverty lines in rural and urban areas are given in Table-2.1. The method of computing the state-specific poverty lines is described below.

The Expert Group disaggregated the national rural poverty line of 1973-74 into state-specific poverty lines using state-specific price indices and inter-state price differential. The state-specific price indices are constructed by averaging the state level commodity group wise indices of Consumer Price Index of Agricultural Labourers (CPIAL) with their respective weights in the consumption basket of the poor at national level in 1973-74. The inter-state price differential is captured by the Fisher's Index. It is a geometric mean of Laspeyres' and Paasche's index and computes the cost of a fixed consumption basket for the states from the quantity and value of consumption of each item. This is a favoured index for such calculation for it satisfies both time reversal tests and factor reversal tests, the two major tests of consistency of index numbers. The state-specific poverty lines of 1973-74 (base year) are updated for use in subsequent years by state-specific price indices.

Table 2.1 : State-Specific Poverty Lines (Rs. monthly per capita).

		Rural		Urban	
S.No.	State	1973-74	1993-94	1973-74	1993-94
0	1	2	3	4	5
1.	Andhra Pradesh	41.71	163.02	53.96	278.14
2.	Assam	49.82	232.05	50.26	212.42
3.	Bihar	57.68	212.16	61.27	238.49
4.	Gujarat	47.10	202.11	62.17	297.22
5.	Haryana	49.95	233.79	52.42	258.23
6.	Himachal Pradesh	49.95	233.79	51.93	253.61
7.	Karnataka	47.24	186.63	58.22	302.89
8.	Kerala	51.68	243.84	62.78	280.54
9.	Madhya Pradesh	50.20	193.10	63.02	317.16
10.	Maharashtra	50.47	194.94	59.48	328.56
11.	Orissa	46.87	194.03	59.34	298.22
12.	Punjab	49.95	233.79	51.93	253.61
13.	Rajasthan	50.96	215.89	59.99	280.85
14.	Tamil Nadu	45.09	196.53	51.54	296.63
15.	Uttar Pradesh	48.92	213.01	57.37	258.65
16.	West Bengal	54.49	220.74	54.81	247.53
	All India	49.63	205.84	56.76	281.35

Source : Planning Commission, Government of India

The methodology of working out state-specific urban poverty

lines is identical to that in rural areas. The national urban poverty line of 1973-74 is disaggregated into state-specific poverty lines using state-specific price indices and inter-state price differential. The state-specific price indices are constructed from the commodity group Consumer Price Index of Industrial Workers (CPIIW), averaged by their respective weights in the consumption basket of the poor at national level in 1973-74. The inter-state price differential is captured through the Fisher's Index.

Poverty Ratio

The state-specific percentage of people below the poverty line (poverty ratio), is estimated from the state-specific poverty lines and distribution of persons by expenditure groups obtained from the NSS data on consumer expenditure. The Expert Group, due to non-availability of state level prices, estimated poverty lines for eighteen States and Union Territories (UTs) and estimated poverty for these States/UTs. The poverty ratio in the remaining States/UTs were equated with one of these 18 States/UTs based on the criteria of physical contiguity of areas and similarity of economic profile. The poverty ratios in rural and urban areas are estimated for the year 1973-74 (base year) and also for the years for which NSS consumer expenditure data from large samples are available. The rural and urban poverty ratios are aggregated to get the poverty ratio for the state as a whole. The all-India poverty ratio is obtained as a weighted average of state-wise poverty ratios. The state-wise poverty ratios in rural and urban areas and for the state as a whole in 16 major states are given in Table-2.2 and the state-wise number of poor in Table-2.3. The poverty scenario at national level in rural and urban areas is given below.

Poverty Ratio and Number of Poor

Year	Rural	Urban	Total
I. 1973-74			
a) Poverty Ratio	56.4	49.0	54.9
b) Number of Poor (million)	261.3	60.0	321.3
II. 1993-94			
a) Poverty Ratio	37.3	32.4	36.0
b) Number of Poor (million)	244.0	76.3	320.3

Table 2.2 : State-Specific Poverty Ratios

		Rural		Urban		Combined	
S.No.	State	1973-74	1993-94	1973-74	1993-94	1973-74	1993-94
0	1	2	3	4	5	6	7
1.	Andhra Pradesh	48.41	15.92	50.61	38.33	48.86	22.19
2.	Assam	52.67	45.01	36.92	7.73	51.21	40.86
3.	Bihar	62.99	58.21	52.95	34.50	61.91	54.96
4.	Gujarat	46.35	22.18	52.57	27.89	48.15	24.21
5.	Haryana	34.23	28.02	40.18	16.38	35.36	25.05
6.	Himachal Pradesh	27.42	30.34	13.17	9.18	26.39	28.44
7.	Karnataka	55.14	29.88	52.53	40.14	54.47	33.16
8.	Kerala	59.19	25.76	62.74	24.55	59.79	25.43
9.	Madhya Pradesh	62.66	40.64	57.65	48.38	61.78	42.52
10.	Maharashtra	57.71	37.93	43.87	35.15	53.24	36.86
11.	Orissa	67.28	49.72	55.62	41.64	66.18	48.56
12.	Punjab	28.21	11.95	27.96	11.35	28.15	11.77
13.	Rajasthan	44.76	26.46	52.13	30.49	46.14	27.41
14.	Tamil Nadu	57.43	32.48	49.40	39.77	54.94	35.03
15.	Uttar Pradesh	56.53	42.28	60.09	35.39	57.07	40.85
16.	West Bengal	73.16	40.80	34.67	22.41	63.43	35.66
	All India	56.44	37.27	49.01	32.36	54.88	35.97

Source : Same as Table 2.1.

The poverty ratio reduced by about one percent point annually between 1973-74 and 1993-94. The decline is more in rural areas (19.1% point) than urban (16.6% point), but the rate of decline is same (2.05% per year) in both the areas. The number of poor as a result of population growth remained stable at around 320 million.

This fact should not over-shadow the 300 million persons who joined the non-poor group during this period, but underlines the need for containment of the growth rate of population.

Table 2.3 : State-Specific Number of Poor *(million)*

		Rural		Urban		Combined	
S.No.	State	1973-74	1993-94	1973-74	1993-94	1973-74	1993-94
0	1	2	3	4	5	6	7
1.	Andhra Pradesh	17.82	7.95	4.75	7.45	22.57	15.40
2.	Assam	7.64	9.43	0.55	0.20	8.18	9.64
3.	Bihar	33.65	45.09	3.41	4.25	37.06	49.34
4.	Gujarat	9.46	6.22	4.36	4.30	13.84	10.52
5.	Haryana	3.01	3.66	0.82	0.73	3.83	4.39
6.	Himachal Pradesh	0.94	1.54	0.04	0.05	0.97	1.59
7.	Karnataka	12.84	9.60	4.23	6.05	17.07	15.65
8.	Kerala	11.14	5.60	2.42	2.05	13.55	7.64
9.	Madhya Pradesh	23.12	21.62	4.51	8.23	27.63	29.85
10.	Maharashtra	21.08	19.33	7.66	11.19	28.74	30.52
11.	Orissa	14.22	14.09	1.22	1.97	15.45	16.06
12.	Punjab	3.05	1.78	1.00	0.74	4.05	2.51
13.	Rajasthan	10.14	9.47	2.71	3.38	12.85	12.85
14.	Tamil Nadu	17.26	12.17	6.69	8.04	23.95	20.21
15.	Uttar Pradesh	45.00	49.62	8.57	10.83	53.57	60.45
16.	West Bengal	25.80	20.99	4.13	4.47	29.93	25.46
	All India	261.29	244.03	60.05	76.34	321.34	320.37

Source : Same as Table 2.1.

State-wise Poverty Ratio

Between 1973-74 and 1993-94, there has been a secular decline in state-wise poverty ratios but not of the number of poor, for which a greater reduction of poverty ratio was needed. The reduction in the poverty ratio was not enough to reduce the number of poor in as many as eight out of these sixteen states. The change in statal poverty from 1973-74 to 1993-94 characterises the following :

(a) The pace of poverty reduction is fast in seven states where the number of poor has declined and that of non-poor increased.
(b) The pace of poverty reduction is moderate in eight states where the number of both poor and non-poor increased.

The combined rural and urban poor in twelve states account for 95% of the country's poor in 1993-94. In six of these twelve states the number of poor reduced between 1973-74 and 1993-94. These are: Andhra Pradesh, Gujarat, Karnataka, Kerala, Tamil Nadu and West Bengal. It remained the same in Rajasthan and increased in the other five states, viz., Bihar, Madhya Pradesh, Maharashtra, Orissa and Uttar Pradesh. The number of rural poor in ten of these twelve states declined. The two states where the number of rural poor did not decline are Bihar and Uttar Pradesh.

The decline in number of rural poor has been spectacular in four southern states, viz., Andhra Pradesh, Karnataka, Kerala and Tamil Nadu. Between 1973-74 and 1993-94, in these four southern states:

(a) Average rural poverty ratio declined from 54.2% to 25%.
(b) Number of rural poor declined from 59.1 million to 35.3 million;
(c) Number of rural non-poor increased from 50 million to 106 million.

For tracking the nature of poverty reduction, the states have been grouped into four categories in terms of their base level rural poverty as follows.

Category I. Bihar, Madhya Pradesh, Orissa, West Bengal.

Category II. Assam, Karnataka, Kerala, Maharashtra, Tamil Nadu, Uttar Pradesh.
Category III. Andhra Pradesh, Gujarat, Rajasthan.
Category IV. Haryana, Himachal Pradesh, Punjab.

The base year (1973-74) rural poverty ratio range from 63 to 73% in category I, 53 to 57% in category II, 44 to 48% in category III and 27 to 34% in category IV states.

Poverty Ratio in Categories of States

Year	Rural	Urban	Total
I.1973-74			
a) Category I	65.97 (1.54)	46.77 (1.43)	62.86 (1.59)
b) Category II	56.69 (2.02)	51.34 (1.86)	55.49 (2.00)
c) Category III	46.85 (3.99)	51.67 (2.23)	47.92 (3.34)
d) Category IV	30.39 (1.80)	31.54 (4.25)	30.63 (2.33)
II. 1993-94			
a) Category I	48.37	35.04	45.65
b) Category II	37.69	35.29	37.02
c) Category III	20.77	32.93	24.27
d) Category IV	21.13	13.22	19.10

N.B.:The figures in brackets are annual average rate of decline of poverty ratio between 1973-74 and 1993-94.

The rate of decline in rural poverty has been fastest in Category III states, where the average level was moderate (44 to 48%) in 1973-74. The rate of decline has been slow in high poverty states, i.e., in Category I, mainly due to lack of growth in income and consumption. The rate of reduction in the urban poverty ratio in Category IV states has been fast.

One way of assessing the relative performance of the states in the poverty eradication is to compare their population share with the share of poor. The four southern states, viz., Andhra Pradesh, Karnataka, Kerala and Tamil Nadu can be labelled with success stories while failure looms large on Bihar, Orissa and Madhy

Pradesh. Against a more or less stable share of rural population, the share of rural poor in the four southern states reduced by 8.1% point (from 22.6% in 1973-74 to 14.5% in 1993-94) whereas in the failed states, i.e., Bihar, Orissa and Madhya Pradesh, the share of rural poor increased by 5.9% point (from 27.2% in 1973-74 to 33.1% in 1993-94).

Growth-Equity Nexus

Poverty ratio is negatively associated with per capita consumption and positively with inequality. As per Central Statistical Organisation (CSO) National Accounts Statistics, per capita real consumption increased by 1.8% per year between 1973-74 and 1993-94. But, these estimates of poverty are based on NSS consumption, whose growth rates are lower than those of CSO consumption. NSS consumption estimates are available only at current prices. Netting out the price rise implicit in the updation of poverty line, the per capita consumption of NSS is observed to rise by 1.24% per year in rural areas and 1.34% per year in urban areas during the period 1973-74 to 1993-94.

Inequality in consumption distribution is measured by the Lorenz ratio, whose value lies between zero and unity. Lorenz ratio closer to zero indicates lesser inequality. At the national level, inequality has not changed significantly since the 1970s. The inequality in the states, however, varies widely. It is generally high in the states with high per capita consumption. The incidence of poverty in these states is low. A few states have low per capita consumption and low inequality, and poverty ratio in these states is high. The pattern of poverty reduction between 1973-74 and 1993-94 in rural areas is:

(a) Increase in per capita consumption contributed to the poverty reduction in Andhra Pradesh and Gujarat.
(b) Increase in per capita consumption and reduction in inequality contributed to the poverty reduction in Karnataka, Kerala and West Bengal.
(c) Poverty reduction in Maharashtra and Tamil Nadu is

exclusively due to rise in per capita consumption as inequality increased.

(d) Rural areas of Bihar, Orissa and to some extent, Madhya Pradesh are circumscribed by low-consumption, low-inequality and high poverty. These states suffer from structural problems for which general development strategies require to be supplemented by special programmes in order to tackle the problem of poverty.

The pattern of poverty reduction in urban areas has been such that:

(a) Increase in both per capita consumption and inequality characterise the poverty reduction in 10 out of these 16 states.

(b) In two states, the decline in urban poverty is exclusively due to rise in per capita consumption.

(c) Rise in per capita consumption and reduction in inequality characterise the poverty reduction in three states.

There has been considerable variation in the reduction of rural and urban poverty in some states mainly due to differential rise in per capita consumption in the two areas. These show:

(a) A faster reduction in rural poverty and a slower reduction in urban poverty is witnessed in Andhra Pradesh, Karnataka, Tamil Nadu and West Bengal.

(b) A slow reduction in urban poverty is accompanied by a slower reduction in rural poverty in Assam, Bihar, Haryana and Uttar Pradesh.

(c) Both rural and urban poverty reduced significantly in Gujarat, Kerala, Punjab and Rajasthan.

The Anti-Poverty Programmes

The reduction in poverty is the outcome of increase in income accruing to the poor from the general growth process and that arising from direct income generation programmes, bypassing the general growth process. Income generation programmes are of two types. The first one relate to creation of assets for generation of a flow of regular income which when added to the income originated from the general growth process, is expected to enable the beneficiaries to cross the poverty line. The second is the employment generation programmes, which enable the beneficiaries to earn wage, in cash, kind or both and raises their consumption level.

The asset generation programme during the period April 1980 to March 1999 was known as the Integrated Rural Development Programme (IRDP). From 1st April, 1999 it was re-named as Swarnjayanti Gram Swarozgar Yojana (SGSY) and the assisted families or groups are called Swarozgaris (self-employeds). The basic objectives of the programme remain unchanged. Investment in IRDP peaked after mid-1980s and per family investment increased by 37% in real terms between the first half of the 1980s (1981-82 to 1985-86) and mid-1990s (1994-95 and 1995-96). Since 1980, the IRDP has assisted about 55 million families. An average of 5.5 persons per family means 300 million persons are covered by IRDP. These numbers in view of the ultimate aim of enabling the families to cross the poverty line are, in fact, misleadingly anodyne. The studies relating to implementation of IRDP show that it has been able to provide additional income to the rural poor. But the extent to which this additionality in income has enabled the beneficiary families to cross the poverty line is not known. There is also a possibility of the beneficiaries sliding back below the poverty line due to non-viability of their assets or lack of after care support. How many of them have been able to sustain the assets are also not precisely known.

The objective of the employment generation programme is to generate sustained and supplementary employment to the rural poor. Unlike the asset generation programme, this has often been change, both in name and content. It began in 1980 with National Rural Employment Programme (NREP), supplemented by Rural Landless Employment Guarantee Programme (RLEGP) in 1983. In 1989, Jawahar Rozgar Yojana (JRY) replaced both NREP and

RLEGP. Employment Assurance Scheme (EAS) was launched in 1993 to cater to the rural poor in backward districts. From 1st April 1999, the nature of EAS was changed and JRY was replaced by Jawahar Gram Samridhi Yojana (JGSY). Finally, in September 2001 both JGSY and EAS were replaced by Sampoorna Grameen Rozgar Yojana (SGRY).

The employment programmes generated on an average 700 million man-days of employment in the second half of the 1980s and 890 million man-days in the first half of the 1990s. The real wage rate (at 1980-81 prices) also increased from Rs. 13 per man-day to Rs. 15 per man-day during the same period. These are averages of all employment programmes and in addition to the wages paid in kind. Employment generation programmes do not permanently allow the poor to cross the poverty line without continuing support of these programmes. But, these programmes can have a tremendous impact on reducing the severity of poverty, as its beneficiaries are the poorest of the poor. In fact, in years of natural calamity such as drought, employment generation programmes have successfully prevented rise in the severity of poverty.

There is no doubt that a significant portion of the poverty reduction since the 1980s has been effected through direct income generation programmes. However, there is a good deal of argument about the number of persons crossing the poverty line entirely as a result of the anti-poverty programmes, at the root of which is an obscure and complex issue of how to calculate the income generation from the operation of these programmes alone.

The Trend of Poverty Indices

The measure of poverty ratio makes no distinction within the broad category of the poor depending upon their actual levels of consumption and deprivation. As a result, the poverty ratio fails to capture the depth and severity of poverty in an adequate manner. A measure for capturing the depth of poverty is the Poverty Gap Ratio (PGR), which adjusts the poverty ratio with the difference between the per capita consumption of the poor and the poverty line expressed as a percentage of the poverty line. It is a measure of the magnitude of the effort required to shift the consumption of all persons below the poverty line to the level of the poverty line. The severity of poverty is captured from an index known as the Squared Poverty Gap (SPG). It is the individual poverty gap raised to the power 2 and derived from a family of index developed by James Foster, Joel Greer and Erik Thorbecke. SPG is composed of poverty ratio and poverty gap ratio, and captures the consumption distribution of the poor as measured by the coefficient of variation. This measure explicitly takes into account the higher intensity of efforts required to address the people who are progressively further below the poverty line in order to bring them above the poverty line. The mathematical scaffolding of the poverty indices and measures derived from them is given in Appendix-I. Table-2.4 gives these poverty indices estimated from the NSS consumer expenditure data.

Until Mid-1960s

During the period 1957-58 to 1960-61, all the three indices of poverty declined. But, from 1960-61, the poverty indices rose steadily until 1966-67. This period was one of the worst for Indian economy as it witnessed two full-scale wars, in October 1962 and September 1965 and three successive years of drought, from 1964-65 to 1966-67. Funding the sinews of war worsened the economic condition. The inability of agriculture to withstand drought resulted in near-famine situation in many parts of rural areas.

Change in Poverty Indices Until Mid-1960s
(per cent per year)

Year	Rural	Urban	Total
I. 1957-58 to 1960-61			
a) Poverty Ratio	-6.28	-2.21	-5.61
b) Poverty Gap Ratio	-10.56	-4.62	-9.61
c) Squared Poverty Gap	-14.28	-5.91	-12.90
II. 1960-61 to 1966-67			
a) Poverty Ratio	5.97	2.65	5.37
b) Poverty Gap Ratio	8.35	3.30	7.47
c) Squared Poverty Gap	10.40	3.56	9.18

Table 2.4 : Poverty Indices

	Year	Poverty Ratio			Poverty Gap Ratio			Squared Poverty Gap		
		Rural	Urban	Total	Rural	Urban	Total	Rural	Urban	Total
	0	1	2	3	4	5	6	7	8	9
1.	1957-58	55.16	47.75	53.84	19.01	15.95	18.47	8.78	7.00	8.46
2.	1960-61	45.40	44.65	45.27	13.60	13.84	13.64	5.53	5.83	5.59
3.	1966-67	64.30	52.24	62.00	22.01	16.81	21.02	10.01	7.19	9.47
4.	1977-78	50.60	40.50	48.36	15.03	11.69	14.28	6.06	4.53	5.72
5.	1983-84	45.31	35.65	43.00	12.65	9.52	11.90	4.84	3.56	4.53
6.	1986-87	38.81	34.29	37.69	10.01	9.10	9.79	3.70	3.40	3.63
7.	1987-88	39.23	36.20	38.47	9.28	9.12	9.24	2.98	3.06	3.00
8.	1988-89	39.06	36.60	38.44	9.50	9.54	9.51	3.29	3.29	3.29
9.	1989-90	34.30	33.40	34.07	7.80	8.51	7.98	2.58	3.04	2.69
10.	1990-91	36.43	32.76	35.49	8.64	8.51	8.61	2.93	3.12	2.98
11.	1991-92	37.42	33.23	36.34	8.29	8.24	8.28	2.68	2.90	2.74
12.	1992-93	43.47	33.73	40.93	10.88	8.82	10.35	3.81	3.19	3.65
13.	1993-94	36.66	30.51	35.04	8.39	7.4i	8.13	2.79	2.42	2.69
14.	1994-95	38.85	34.23	37.60	8.63	8.85	8.69	2.76	3.17	2.87
15.	1995-96	38.30	30.05	36.05	8.34	7.20	8.03	2.68	2.48	2.62
16.	1996-97	38.46	33.97	37.22	9.03	8.62	8.92	3.17	3.18	3.17

Source : World Bank

Rural poverty ratio between 1960-61 and 1966-67 rose by 20% points and all the three poverty indices reached its peak in 1966-67. The severity of poverty rose faster as the drought prolonged. The rate of increase of SPG, which was twice of that of poverty ratio in the first two years of drought, became three times in the third year. The poverty indices rose faster in rural areas as compared to urban.

Post 1966-67 Phase

The annual average decline in poverty ratio between 1966-67 and 1996-97 is 1.86% in rural areas and 1.67% in urban areas. The trend rates of decline of the poverty indices are similar in rural and urban areas until 1977-78 after which the rates of decline are faster in rural areas.

The poverty indices began declining from 1967-68, the first year of normal monsoon after the unprecedented drought. Rural poverty ratio declined until 1986-87. However, the planning and development strategy failed to make a dent in rural poverty after1986-87, as the poverty ratio remained at the same level even after ten years. Urban poverty ratio declined until 1983-84, and remained at 30 to 35% during the next 15 years i.e., until 1996-97. The poverty gap ratio declined sharply from 1966-67 to 1986-87, but remained at the same level until 1992-93. The decline in the poverty gap ratio has been faster than poverty ratio. But the brighter side of the picture is the decline of SPG by a rate, faster than both poverty ratio and poverty gap ratio. The rural employment programmes and the specific measures to rush additional quantities of foodgrain in drought years (for example, 1987-88) prevented rise in the severity of poverty in rural areas. The underlining feature of poverty reduction in recent times is the faster reduction in the depth and severity of poverty and over time there has been a trend towards a greater degree of clustering of the poor around the poverty line leading to a situation where economic growth is likely to have a considerably larger impact on poverty reduction than before. This would of course require that the measures of relative inequality do not deteriorate sufficiently to off-set the growth effect.

Decline in Poverty Indices Since Mid-1960s
(per cent per year)

Period	Rural	Urban	Total
I.1966-67 to 1977-78			
a) Poverty Ratio	2.04	2.11	2.11
b) Poverty Gap Ratio	3.28	3.29	3.35
c) Squared Poverty Gap	4.31	4.40	4.40
II. 1977-78 to 1996-97			
a) Poverty Ratio	1.32	1.17	1.33
b) Poverty Gap Ratio	2.83	1.89	2.67
c) Squared Poverty Gap	3.88	2.35	3.57
III.1966-67 to 1996-97			
a) Poverty Ratio	1.86	1.67	1.87
b) Poverty Gap Ratio	3.29	2.50	3.17
c) Squared Poverty Gap	4.39	3.16	4.17

Impact of Economic Reforms

There has been a good deal of debate on economic reforms and liberalisation affecting poverty reduction. The reform process began in July 1991, when the economy was in the midst of a series of crises. Mainly as a result, the rural poverty ratio in 1992-93 rose by 6% points. But in the following year (1993-94), the upturn was reversed and poverty ratio went back to its earlier value.

The behaviour of the long-term trend rate of decline in the indices of poverty can be a route to assess the impact of economic reform and liberalisation on poverty reduction. The long-term trend is first worked out for the period 1966-67 to 1986-87. Thereafter, the trend growth rates are calculated by adding each successive year. Estimated this way, the long-term trend rate of decline of rural poverty ratio remains above the trend until 1989-90 and lowers gradually from 1991-92. Poverty gap ratio and SPG display a similar behaviour with the exception that their rates of decline do not reduce until 1992-93. The trend in urban areas is somewhat different. It remains stable until 1996-97. The nature of the trend is similar in case of poverty gap ratio but not in case of SPG, which slowed down (from 1988-89) before the liberalisation process began. In the 1990s, the poverty ratio and the poverty gap ratio in rural areas did not fall after 1993-94. The SPG did not rise after 1986-87, except for 1992-93. Thus, the process of economic reforms and liberalisation might have temporarily raised the poverty ratio but not the severity of poverty.

The Pace of Decline in Poverty Indices

The pace of decline in the poverty indices during the last three decades is assessed using econometric method.

Between 1957-58 and 1996-97, the poverty indices could be computed for 28 points of time for which NSS consumption expenditure data are available. The trend rate of decline in the poverty indices, calculated in terms of a moving average using exponential time function do not show either rising or falling trend until 1963-64. Between 1964-65 and 1996-97, the trend rates are computed for 12 periods. Each of these 12 periods contain eleven observations and all excepting the last two represent 20 years. For the sake of uniformity, the last two periods are excluded and the rate of decline is computed for 10 periods, each representing 20 years. The rate of decline of the poverty indices for these ten periods, covering thirty years, 1964-65 to 1994-95, is given in Table-2.5.

A linear time trend of these trend rates (of the poverty indices) in urban areas yield negative and statistically significant regression coefficients. These indicate deceleration in the rates of decline of the poverty indices in urban areas, and judging the results, the deceleration appears to be quite strong in case of poverty gap ratio and SPG. In rural areas, the regression coefficients of the linear time trend do not turn out to be statistically significant. Alternatively, quadratic trend equations show:(a) positive sign of the coefficient of time and negative sign of the coefficient of square of time, (b) statistically significant regression parameters and (c) high value of coefficient of determination. These can be used to infer that the rates of decline in the poverty indices in rural areas increased

Table 2.5 : Decline in Poverty Indices

(Percent per year)

Period	Poverty Ratio			Poverty Gap Ratio			Squared Poverty Gap		
	Rural	Urban	Total	Rural	Urban	Total	Rural	Urban	Total
0	1	2	3	4	5	6	7	8	9
1. 1964-65 to 1983-84	1.39	1.97	1.54	2.10	2.94	2.31	2.73	3.68	2.97
2. 1965-66 to 1986-87	2.03	2.12	2.10	3.11	3.07	3.16	3.94	3.74	3.96
3. 1966-67 to 1987-88	2.23	1.94	2.22	3.64	2.95	3.55	4.83	3.81	4.68
4. 1967-68 to 1988-89	2.19	1.77	2.15	3.60	2.71	3.46	4.76	3.56	4.57
5. 1968-69 to 1989-90	2.29	1.70	2.21	3.75	2.59	3.54	4.93	3.36	4.63
6. 1969-70 to 1990-91	2.31	1.70	2.23	3.79	2.49	3.55	4.98	3.13	4.62
7. 1970-71 to 1991-92	2.29	1.69	2.20	3.88	2.48	3.61	5.13	3.08	4.73
8. 1972-73 to 1992-93	2.11	1.74	2.07	3.72	2.46	3.49	5.00	2.98	4.61
9. 1973-74 to 1993-94	2.07	1.82	2.05	3.69	2.56	3.48	4.93	3.18	4.60
10. 1977-78 to 1994-95	1.63	1.23	1.59	3.33	1.97	3.07	4.64	2.61	4.21

N.B.: 1. The rates of decline are estimated from exponential time function.
2. The R-bar square of the equations exceed 0.9 in all the cases.

in the initial stages and decreased thereafter. The poverty indices for the country as a whole follow the trend in rural areas. Table-2.6 gives these equations.

Table 2.6 : Pace of Change of Poverty Indices : 1964-65 to 1994-95

Dependent Variable	Constant	Independent Variables		R^{-2}
		Time	Square of Time	
1. **Poverty Ratio**				
Rural	1.16	0.4239 (-7.2)	-0.0373 (7.2)	0.85
Urban	2.10	-0.0606 (3.5)		0.55
Total	1.38	0.3313 (5.5)	-0.0304 (5.7)	0.77
2. **Poverty Gap Ratio**				
Rural	1.77	0.6736 (6.9)	-0.0522 (6.0)	0.85
Urban	3.14	-0.0942 (5.7)		0.78
Total	2.09	0.5164 (5.7)	-0.0419 (5.2)	0.79
3. **Squared Poverty Gap**				
Rural	2.28	.0.8742 (6.6)	-0.0651 (5.5)	0.86
Urban	3.96	-0.1174 (6.7)		0.83
Total	2.67	0.6784 (5.6)	-0.0530 (5.0)	0.80

N.B. : 1. Estimated from the annual rate of decline given in Table 2.5.
2. Figures in the parenthesis contain t-values.

The likely impact of economic reforms on the long run trend of poverty indices, assessed following the same route indicates acceleration in the rate of decline of the poverty indices particularly of SPG in rural areas and its deceleration in urban areas. The acceleration in the rate of decline of poverty indices in rural areas is lost after 1990-91. Perhaps, this is the major conclusion regarding liberalisation affecting the average level and the rate of reduction of poverty. All said and done, the decline in the mean level of poverty by about 30% points in 30 years (1966-67 to 1995-96) and its ability to come out of the cyclics of agricultural production, are no mean achievements of the planning and development strategy. The faster decline in SPG since the mid-1980s underlines the impact of the process of development in recent years more on severity of poverty.

The NSS data are not available for all the years and so also the estimates of poverty. This leaves a few peaks and troughs beyond the scope of the analysis. For example, the impact of oil shock of 1978-79 and the drought in 1979-80, which caused the agricultural production to decline by 12.3%, the maximum since independence, go beyond the scope of assessment. Also excluded are exceptionally good agricultural years such as 1975-76 and 1980-81, when agricultural output increased by more than 10%. These are undoubtedly the years with low poverty.

3

CONSUMPTION AND POVERTY BY CLASS

The per capita consumption and incidence of poverty are assessed for major occupation and socio-economic groups and for gender and religion of the population in order to gather a fair idea about their levels of living. The impact of family size and land possession on levels of living are also examined to explore the efficacy of small family norm and of equity in land distribution.

Occupation

In rural areas, the households are classified into four groups in terms of their means of livelihood as (a) Agricultural Labourers (AL), (b) Other Labourers (OL), (c) Self-Employed in Agriculture (SEA), (d) Self-Employed in Non-Agriculture (SENA), with the fifth as those not covered by any of these occupation groups as Others (OHH). Manual labour in agriculture and/or non-agricultural occupation in return for wages and salaries in cash or kind is defined as rural labour. The rural labour households earning more than half of their income from wage paid manual labour in agriculture are defined as agricultural labour household. The remaining rural labour households, i.e., those households earning less than half of their income from wage paid manual labour are called other labour households. Persons who are engaged in their own farms or non-farm enterprises are called self-employed. If more than half of the income is earned from self-employment in agricultural occupation, the households are categorised as self-employed in agriculture and if more than half of the income of the family is generated outside agricultural operations, the households are classified as self-employed in non-agriculture.

In urban areas, the households are classified into three groups as (a) Self-Employed (SE), (b) Regular Wages and Salary Earners (RW&SE) and (c) Casual Labourers (CL) depending on their major source of income from gainful employment in the occupation, with the fourth as those not covered by any of these groups (OHH). The occupation group of the household is identified from the highest income earned from the sources mentioned in (a) to (c) above.

Table-3.1 gives the occupation group-wise percentage of persons as estimated from the NSS data. At the national level, Self Employed in Agriculture in rural areas and Regular Wage and Salary Earners in urban areas account for nearly 40% of the population in the respective areas. The dispersion of occupation specific percentage of persons among the states is low in major occupation groups. The average and variation in the percentage of persons in each occupation groups along with their maximum and minimum are given below.

State-wise Variation in Occupation-Specific Distribution of Persons

	Maximum	Minimum	Average	Variation
I. Rural				
1. SENA	W.B. (20.5)	M.P.(6.2)	12.6	27
2. AL	T.N. (40.9)	H.P. (2.5)	27.6	31
3. OL	Kerala (18.2)	Bihar (3.2)	7.3	51
4. SEA	H.P. (63.2)	Kerala (20.9)	41.2	30
5. OHH	Maharashtra (24.4)	M.P. (4.8)	11.3	49
II. Urban				
1. SE	U.P. (53.4)	H.P. (25.6)	37.1	17
2. RW&SE	Maharashtra (51.0)	Kerala (28.8)	42.7	14
3. CL	Kerala (31.4)	Assam (6.3)	12.9	47
4. OHH	H. P. (21.1)	Punjab (3.7)	7.3	42

Table 3.1 : Distribution of Persons by Occupation Groups

		Rural					Urban			
S.No.	States	SENA	AL	OL	SEA	OHH	SE	RW & SE	CL	OHH
0	1	2	3	4	5	6	7	8	9	10
1.	Andhra Pradesh	12.8	35.8	6.1	27.3	18.0	33.0	39.1	16.0	11.9
2.	Assam	11.8	20.2	10.3	45.8	11.9	41.0	45.9	6.3	6.8
3.	Bihar	11.6	35.2	3.2	41.4	8.7	39.6	38.8	11.6	10.0
4.	Gujarat	8.5	32.6	8.1	30.3	20.5	32.4	41.1	11.4	15.1
5.	Haryana	16.4	15.4	12.3	43.8	12.0	42.1	41.4	11.3	5.2
6.	Himachal Pradesh	10.7	2.5	11.9	63.2	11.7	25.6	46.6	6.7	21.1
7.	Karnataka	13.0	34.9	3.6	41.5	6.9	36.3	41.9	16.0	5.8
8.	Kerala	14.7	24.0	18.2	20.9	22.2	34.2	28.8	31.4	5.6
9.	Madhya Pradesh	6.2	30.9	4.4	53.7	4.8	36.6	45.8	12.6	5.0
10.	Maharashtra	7.7	31.6	7.4	28.9	24.4	32.5	51.0	9.6	6.8
11.	Orissa	14.9	33.4	4.6	38.8	8.3	30.8	48.9	10.5	9.8
12.	Punjab	16.1	26.2	6.7	36.6	14.4	49.2	38.7	8.4	3.7
13.	Rajasthan	11.2	8.6	15.1	57.7	7.4	44.5	41.5	7.1	6.9
14.	Tamil Nadu	13.5	40.9	12.5	23.0	10.1	32.5	40.9	20.5	6.0
15.	Uttar Pradesh	13.5	17.6	4.9	57.7	6.3	53.4	31.3	10.5	4.8
16.	West Bengal	20.5	30.1	9.6	31.3	8.5	36.3	47.8	10.7	5.2
17.	All India	12.6	27.6	7.3	41.2	11.3	37.1	42.7	12.9	7.3

N.B.: SENA=Self Employed in Non-Agriculture, AL=Agricultural Labourer, OL=Other Labour, SEA=Self Employed in Agriculture, SE=Self-Employed, RW&SE=Regular Wage and Salary Earners, CL=Casual Labourer, OHH=Other Households

Table 3.2 : Consumption and Poverty by Occupation Groups

	SENA	AL	OL	SEA	OHH	ALL
1	2	3	4	5	6	7
I. Rural						
1.Per Capita Monthly Consumption (Rs.)						
(a) Bottom 30%	150.01	97.26	138.44	156.70	183.07	149.52
(b) Middle 40%	254.22	194.07	230.58	260.37	324.71	239.96
(c) Top 30%	495.15	368.70	443.23	502.84	664.64	468.53
(d) All	295.24	217.41	266.74	302.01	384.20	281.40
2.Inequality (Lorenz Ratio)	0.2744	0.2379	0.2616	0.2720	0.2976	0.2816
3.Poverty						
(a) Very Poor	11.08	27.17	14.55	9.96	6.76	15.26
(b) Moderately Poor	21.14	29.58	25.14	19.23	10.82	21.97
(c) Poor	32.21	56.75	39.69	29.19	17.57	37.23
(d) Lower Non-Poor	36.13	30.10	36.10	37.57	30.74	34.19
(e) Upper Non-Poor	31.66	13.15	24.21	33.24	51.68	28.58
(f) Non-Poor	67.79	43.25	60.31	70.81	82.43	62.77
II. Urban	SE	RW&SE	CL	OHH	ALL	
1.Per Capita Monthly Consumption (Rs.)						
(a) Bottom 30%	179.57	239.65	96.03	196.31	206.86	
(b) Middle 40%	345.60	431.28	247.21	422.26	364.00	
(c) Top 30%	786.15	957.56	497.67	1025.62	834.48	
(d) All	427.96	531.68	276.99	535.48	458.05	
2.Inequality (Lorenz Ratio)	0.3272	0.3274	0.2474	0.3664	0.3400	
3.Poverty						
(a) Very Poor	15.75	7.31	35.81	11.55	14.85	
(b) Moderately Poor	20.44	13.62	26.84	14.93	17.42	
(c) Poor	36.19	20.93	62.64	26.48	32.28	
(d) Lower Non-Poor	29.70	29.27	25.83	24.53	28.83	
(e) Upper Non-Poor	34.11	49.80	11.52	48.99	38.89	
(f) Non-Poor	63.81	79.07	37.36	73.52	67.72	

N.B.: Legends in Table 3.1.

Broadly, the percentage of population engaged in AL and SEA in a state are inversely related. Also, the percentage of persons engaged as CL in a state is inversely related with SE and RW&SE. The rank correlation coefficient between AL and SEA is -0.56 and that between SE and CL and between RW&SE and CL is -0.41. Per capita consumption and poverty by occupation groups in rural and urban areas at national level are given in Table-3.2.

Consumption and Poverty by Occupation

The relative well being or deprivation of the occupation groups can be traced by comparing their consumption with the national average. The agricultural labourers in rural areas and casual labourers in urban areas are worse-off as their per capita consumption is least among all the occupation groups. The relative inequality as measured by the Lorenz ratio of per capita consumption distribution is also least for these two groups. Occupation-wise, per capita consumption and Lorenz ratio are positively related. However, fractile–specific disparity in per capita consumption across the occupation groups is similar. The hierarchy within the occupation does not get altered as the chances of a poor becoming less poor remain remote in the absence of occupational switching, thus making occupation the prime determinant of the level of living.

In rural areas, the poverty ratio among the agricultural labourers (56.8%) is three times of that of others (17.6%). In urban areas, the poverty ratio among the casual labourers (62.6%) is three times of that of regular wage and salary earners (20.9%). Similar differences exist in case of the percentage of very poor and also of the percentage of upper group of non-poor. Persons with consumption less than three-fourth of the poverty line are defined as very poor and those with per capita consumption exceeding one and a half times of the poverty line are defined as upper group of non-poor. The high poverty ratio among the agricultural labourers and casual labourers is the outcome of low consumption and low inequality whereas the low poverty among others is the outcome of high consumption and high inequality.

Table 3.3 : State-wise Poverty Ratio by Occupation Groups

		Rural					Urban			
S.No.	States	SENA	AL	OL	SEA	OHH	SE	RW&SE	CL	OHH
0	1	2	3	4	5	6	7	8	9	10
1.	Andhra Pradesh	9.38	22.67	19.64	11.17	12.44	40.58	25.34	67.15	36.14
2.	Assam	36.37	64.82	69.13	38.25	22.16	6.63	5.72	35.89	2.19
3.	Bihar	54.78	77.55	66.41	45.67	42.36	41.37	19.95	69.46	24.47
4.	Gujarat	20.54	33.74	24.54	12.89	16.85	23.56	20.08	54.81	38.43
5.	Haryana	24.85	58.24	42.92	18.29	12.09	17.47	11.58	35.39	4.10
6.	Himachal Pradesh	23.42	50.99	44.65	31.26	10.95	13.34	3.18	40.81	7.48
7.	Karnataka	27.80	46.25	25.64	20.94	7.75	44.01	25.78	72.84	29.95
8.	Kerala	22.44	37.21	32.59	14.67	19.00	22.07	15.98	37.51	10.83
9.	Madhya Pradesh	33.32	59.53	45.06	32.64	17.03	53.60	36.37	79.22	40.61
10.	Maharashtra	24.36	58.12	33.98	25.32	32.08	39.22	25.51	81.19	21.57
11.	Orissa	44.62	67.72	56.39	40.68	27.03	54.96	26.94	74.07	39.02
12.	Punjab	8.46	29.33	18.94	2.23	3.19	10.79	7.61	30.39	15.23
13.	Rajasthan	23.84	42.15	48.20	19.39	21.64	34.23	22.57	59.26	24.78
14.	Tamil Nadu	20.73	48.66	24.11	22.97	15.57	37.49	27.83	65.84	44.54
15.	Uttar Pradesh	44.01	63.90	51.34	36.33	26.39	40.18	18.22	66.19	26.18
16.	West Bengal	35.87	59.90	57.88	28.51	11.28	28.46	11.56	53.27	16.45
17.	All India	32.21	56.75	39.69	29.19	17.57	36.19	20.93	62.64	26.48

N.B.: Legends in Table-3.1.

Occupation specific poverty ratios in the states are given in Table-3.3. These are estimated from the occupation specific consumption distribution (as obtained from the NSS data on consumer expenditure of the large survey of 1993-94) and the state-specific poverty line (as used for all population). The phenomenon of a high poverty ratio among the agricultural labourers in rural areas and casual labourers in urban areas at national level is evident at the state level as well. Poverty ratio among the agricultural labourers is high in Bihar (77.6%), Orissa (67.7%), Assam (64.8%) and Uttar Pradesh (63.9%). The poverty ratio among the casual labourers is about 70% or more in Bihar, Karnataka, Madhya Pradesh, Maharashtra and Orissa. In Andhra Pradesh, 22.2% of the people are poor. But, the poverty ratio among the casual labourers is as high as 67.15%. The poverty ratio in the states is low among the Self Employed in Agriculture in rural areas and Regular Wage and Salary Earners in urban areas.

The relative intensity of poverty among the occupation groups measured by the percentage of very poor is given in Table-3.4. In order to assess the percentage of well-off people, relatively speaking, the percentage of upper group of non-poor are estimated in Table-3.5. In rural areas, the percentage of very poor in Self Employed in Agriculture is relatively low and in 12 of the 16 states, it is less than the national average (40%). It is high in Bihar, Madhya Pradesh, Orissa and Uttar Pradesh. In urban areas, the percentage of very poor is relatively low among the Regular Wage and Salary Earners and high among the Casual Labourers.

Correlation Between Population Groups

	Poverty Ratio and Very Poor	Poverty Ratio and Upper Non-Poor	Very Poor and Upper Non-Poor
I. Rural			
1. SENA	0.91	- 0.94	- 0.80
2. AL	0.95	- 0.93	- 0.80
3. OL	0.95	- 0.97	- 0.89
4. SEA	0.87	- 0.95	- 0.74
II. Urban			
1. SE	0.98	- 0.96	- 0.91
2. RW&SE	0.97	- 0.97	- 0.92
3. CL	0.95	- 0.94	- 0.83

Table 3.4 : State-wise Very Poor by Occupation Groups

(per cent)

S.No.	States	Rural SENA	AL	OL	SEA	OHH	Urban SE	RW&SE	CL	OHH
0	1	2	3	4	5	6	7	8	9	10
1.	Andhra Pradesh	2.28	6.30	5.57	2.43	3.33	17.29	8.14	36.65	16.80
2.	Assam	9.96	25.71	30.49	5.58	7.44	–	–	–	–
3.	Bihar	22.71	44.75	31.69	16.30	17.93	16.39	6.09	37.44	9.51
4.	Gujarat	2.34	10.92	8.35	3.77	4.70	7.90	6.42	27.70	18.70
5.	Haryana	7.28	32.30	10.12	3.00	3.93	4.15	4.08	12.94	2.52
6.	Himachal Pradesh	2.76	20.79	19.33	8.33	3.31	3.04	0.01	4.98	0.02
7.	Karnataka	9.69	21.58	7.50	4.30	3.00	26.20	10.89	43.60	18.06
8.	Kerala	6.56	16.08	11.53	3.94	6.69	8.02	6.76	16.56	4.08
9.	Madhya Pradesh	14.11	27.77	20.42	12.04	5.32	28.33	16.47	54.71	16.11
10.	Maharashtra	10.21	26.69	9.96	9.39	14.11	20.91	11.45	57.27	7.96
11.	Orissa	14.94	34.49	26.06	15.95	7.43	31.21	12.88	51.81	16.73
12.	Punjab	3.08	7.87	3.02	0.27	1.00	2.02	0.52	9.65	5.82
13.	Rajasthan	6.12	22.53	16.67	5.09	6.84	15.47	8.74	24.40	10.61
14.	Tamil Nadu	8.42	20.43	6.77	7.42	6.14	17.19	10.25	34.81	29.45
15.	Uttar Pradesh	19.59	37.25	22.96	14.35	13.66	17.91	6.15	44.45	15.52
16.	West Bengal	9.85	25.50	18.06	5.73	3.36	8.99	3.32	21.73	6.49
17.	All India	11.08	27.17	14.55	9.96	6.76	15.75	7.31	35.81	11.55

N.B.: Legends in Table-3.1

Table 3.5 : State-wise Upper Non-Poor by Occupation Groups

(per cent)

		Rural					Urban			
S.No.	States	SENA	AL	OL	SEA	OHH	SE	RW&SE	CL	OHH
0	1	2	3	4	5	6	7	8	9	10
1.	Andhra Pradesh	55.50	33.97	42.02	59.30	55.82	30.36	44.64	9.29	38.14
2.	Assam	18.15	5.23	3.48	12.55	32.30	53.34	75.69	20.15	77.74
3.	Bihar	13.78	3.41	6.71	16.89	23.52	23.97	46.48	10.83	47.52
4.	Gujarat	46.96	23.43	44.04	48.26	47.14	38.84	44.27	12.30	32.66
5.	Haryana	39.37	19.56	21.08	50.41	58.40	50.68	61.83	31.24	74.61
6.	Himachal Pradesh	38.86	16.30	20.07	33.47	56.44	52.64	78.84	22.02	66.18
7.	Karnataka	36.58	19.20	32.53	40.78	63.67	28.78	44.91	7.65	46.60
8.	Kerala	43.05	22.72	28.89	57.19	50.09	48.19	55.58	22.90	59.32
9.	Madhya Pradesh	36.36	12.31	22.61	29.60	51.26	18.95	31.43	5.02	33.22
10.	Maharashtra	38.72	13.80	30.09	35.75	40.02	37.05	47.17	5.73	47.56
11.	Orissa	17.34	6.30	18.13	20.82	38.76	20.44	43.18	8.83	31.55
12.	Punjab	48.61	23.42	35.89	77.08	63.98	61.97	65.31	33.60	63.81
13.	Rajasthan	36.78	26.83	20.63	42.20	50.15	32.14	46.26	14.80	40.17
14.	Tamil Nadu	45.10	16.33	36.51	36.02	60.25	31.45	41.95	7.69	35.64
15.	Uttar Pradesh	23.44	10.61	15.10	29.41	42.10	28.06	52.28	10.46	53.82
16.	West Bengal	23.32	8.81	11.59	26.71	52.32	41.88	62.58	13.88	61.34
17.	All India	31.66	13.15	24.21	33.24	51.68	34.11	49.80	11.52	48.99

N.B.: Legends in Table-3.1

A positive association between the percentage of poor and very poor, and a negative association between (a) poor and upper group of non-poor and (b) very poor and upper group of non-poor, is witnessed for all the occupation groups, as can be seen from the correlation between population groups given above. Across the states, there is considerable directional similarity in the poverty ratio among SEA with that of SENA and AL, and that among the SE with RW&SE and CL.

Variation in Statal Poverty

(per cent)

	Poverty Ratio	Very Poor	Upper Non-Poor	Percentage of Persons
I.Rural				
1. SENA	43	62	34	27
2. AL	29	43	50	40
3. OL	38	56	48	49
4. SEA	46	65	43	31
II. Urban				
1. SE	45	66	33	19
2. RW&SE	47	66	24	14
3. CL	28	58	58	48

Destitution is uniform across states. Inter-state variation in poverty ratio measured by coefficient of variation given above is found to be less in case of the poorest occupation groups (Agricultural Labourers and Casual Labourers) and high in case of the relatively better-off groups (SEA and RW&SE). The greater inter-state disparity in the percentage of very poor indicates the differential impact of the development process on acute poverty.

Socio-Economic Groups

The level of living of Scheduled Castes (SC) and Scheduled Tribes (ST) and particularly their vicissitudes is watched with great interest. Per capita consumption and poverty indices for these two groups and also for the remaining population, termed here as "others", are estimated from NSS data on consumer expenditure. As these data are not stratified by socio-economic groups, their sample proportions in the NSS, mainly in order to indicate their representativeness, are given below.

Sample Proportion by Socio-Economic Groups

(per cent)

	Rural	Urban	Total
1 .Scheduled Tribe	10.82	3.39	8.98
2. Scheduled Caste	21.10	13.86	19.31
3. ST + SC	31.92	17.25	28.29
4. Others	68.08	82.75	71.71

The sample proportions are not different from the aggregates obtained from the 1991 Census. Per capita consumption and poverty for Scheduled Castes, Scheduled Tribes and others in rural and urban areas at national level are given in Table-3.6.

Consumption and Poverty by Socio-Economic Groups

The per capita consumption of Scheduled Castes and Scheduled Tribes in rural areas is about three-fourth of that of the others. Their consumption distributions are more equal than others. In urban areas, the higher per capita consumption of Scheduled Tribes as compared to the Scheduled Castes is indeed significant in the context of their entry into the mainstream of the economy.

The poverty ratio among the Scheduled Tribes and Scheduled Castes is more than that of the others. The high poverty ratio of the Scheduled Castes and Scheduled Tribes is the outcome of lower per capita consumption and low inequality, while the low poverty ratio among others is mainly on account of high per capita consumption as inequality takes a backseat.

State-wise poverty ratios among the Scheduled Caste and Scheduled Tribes are given in Table-3.7. These are reflective of the scenario that is obtained for all population. In Bihar and Orissa, more than 70% of the rural population of these two groups is poor. State-wise percentage of very poor of these two groups given in Table-3.8 shows a fair amount of similarity in the relative position

Table 3.6 : Consumption and Poverty by Socio Economic Groups

	ST	SC	OHH	ALL
1	2	3	4	5
I. Rural				
1.Per Capita Monthly Consumption (Rs.)				
(a) Bottom 30%	99.66	112.40	149.45	149.52
(b) Middle 40%	204.67	211.09	257.56	239.96
(c) Top 30%	408.69	402.52	514.08	468.53
(d) All	234.37	238.91	302.08	281.40
2.Inequality (Lorenz Ratio)	0.2645	0.2517	0.2834	0.2816
3.Poverty				
(a) Very Poor	24.77	21.79	11.45	15.26
(b) Moderately Poor	27.20	26.54	19.97	21.97
(c) Poor	51.96	48.32	31.43	37.23
(d) Lower Non-Poor	31.57	33.67	35.38	34.19
(e) Upper Non-Poor	16.47	18.01	33.21	28.58
(f) Non-Poor	48.04	51.68	68.57	62.77
II. Urban				
1.Per Capita Monthly Consumption (Rs.)				
(a) Bottom 30%	155.49	131.43	199.63	206.86
(b) Middle 40%	316.54	286.35	384.79	364.00
(c) Top 30%	690.93	627.35	888.26	834.48
(d) All	380.54	342.18	480.28	458.05
2.Inequality (Lorenz Ratio)	0.3067	0.3014	0.3386	0.3400
3.Poverty				
(a) Very Poor	20.06	25.67	12.42	14.85
(b) Moderately Poor	20.67	24.17	17.03	17.42
(c) Poor	40.74	49.84	29.44	32.28
(d) Lower Non-Poor	30.21	28.98	28.58	28.83
(e) Upper Non-Poor	29.05	21.18	41.98	38.89
(f) Non-Poor	59.26	50.16	70.56	67.72

Table 3.7 : State-wise Poverty Ratio by Socio Economic Groups

		Rural		Urban	
S.No.	State	ST	SC	ST	SC
0	1	2	3	4	5
1.	Andhra Pradesh	25.62	26.01	46.51	43.89
2.	Assam	42.21	45.29	7.07	14.32
3.	Bihar	69.96	70.92	35.78	55.04
4.	Gujarat	31.11	32.20	35.55	44.86
5.	Haryana	41.50	46.55	–	23.58
6.	Himachal Pradesh	64.05	36.78	–	18.60
7.	Karnataka	37.52	46.62	62.14	61.60
8.	Kerala	37.30	36.28	1.14	31.70
9.	Madhya Pradesh	56.90	46.00	65.41	65.02
10.	Maharashtra	50.77	51.70	60.95	52.61
11.	Orissa	71.51	49.06	64.80	47.51
12.	Punjab	26.85	21.83	-	27.99
13.	Rajasthan	46.20	38.33	13.19	48.68
14.	Tamil Nadu	44.41	44.14	30.10	61.49
15.	Uttar Pradesh	37.04	59.27	36.89	58.02
16.	West Bengal	62.03	45.28	19.41	37.56
17.	All India	51.96	48.32	40.74	49.84

Table 3.8 : State-wise Very Poor by Socio Economic Groups (per cent)

		Rural		Urban	
S.No.	States	ST	SC	ST	SC
0	1	2	3	4	5
1.	Andhra Pradesh	7.42	7.37	27.95	22.70
2.	Assam	7.54	12.19	–	–
3.	Bihar	38.68	38.80	12.07	27.39
4.	Gujarat	11.08	12.47	14.89	22.03
5.	Haryana	37.10	17.88	–	7.50
6.	Himachal Pradesh	20.22	12.90	–	3.73
7.	Karnataka	17.99	23.28	41.28	38.83
8.	Kerala	21.78	14.84	–	16.13
9.	Madhya Pradesh	28.26	18.09	38.20	40.20
10.	Maharashtra	21.95	24.25	36.05	33.68
11.	Orissa	39.95	19.98	43.51	25.33
12.	Punjab	12.56	5.61	–	6.36
13.	Rajasthan	16.45	15.56	4.49	21.06
14.	Tamil Nadu	18.28	18.22	13.48	34.05
15.	Uttar Pradesh	21.90	31.31	5.84	30.19
16.	West Bengal	16.67	16.46	5.81	16.47
17.	All India	24.77	21.79	20.06	25.67

of the states with that of poverty ratio. The percentage of upper group of non-poor among the Scheduled Castes and Scheduled Tribes, given in Table-3.9 reveal that in two states in rural areas viz., Andhra Pradesh and Punjab, and six in urban areas viz., Assam, Haryana, Himachal Pradesh, Kerala, Punjab and West Bengal, at least 30% of the Scheduled Castes are in the upper group of non-poor. Inter-state variation in poverty ratio among the Scheduled Castes and Scheduled Tribes show a lower variation in case of poverty ratio and percentage of very poor as compared to that of all population indicating a uniform spread of poverty among the SC/STs in the states.

Table 3.9 : State-wise Upper Non-Poor by Socio Economic Groups *(Percentage)*

		Rural		Urban	
S.No.	States	ST	SC	ST	SC
0	1	2	3	4	5
1.	Andhra Pradesh	37.59	32.32	26.05	23.14
2.	Assam	10.10	10.07	70.88	45.26
3.	Bihar	8.48	4.91	25.46	17.83
4.	Gujarat	29.61	27.96	23.31	20.84
5.	Haryana	21.29	20.61	45.70	39.96
6.	Himachal Pradesh	11.58	26.46	–	50.74
7.	Karnataka	21.18	21.40	15.11	11.20
8.	Kerala	31.62	18.22	81.22	30.13
9.	Madhya Pradesh	12.49	19.70	13.10	11.24
10.	Maharashtra	18.01	18.14	18.79	21.45
11.	Orissa	6.87	14.41	15.83	20.30
12.	Punjab	41.02	32.32	49.05	39.67
13.	Rajasthan	19.33	28.02	43.45	20.30
14.	Tamil Nadu	25.12	20.51	40.33	13.60
15.	Uttar Pradesh	30.40	13.21	14.30	15.50
16.	West Bengal	9.05	15.32	54.93	34.54
17.	All India	16.47	18.01	29.05	21.18

Variation in Statal Poverty of SC and ST *(Percentage)*

	Poverty Ratio	Very Poor	Upper Non-Poor
I. Rural			
1.Scheduled Caste	30	47	50
2. Scheduled Tribe	27	45	37
3. All Population	44	65	45
II. Urban			
1. Schedule Caste	36	56	47
2. All Population	44	63	39

Occupation and Socio-Economic Groups

Both occupation and socio-economic groups in India are instant reflection of the levels of living. Precisely for this reason, an assessment of consumption and poverty by cross-classifying occupation and socio-economic groups becomes important for closely targeting the poor. The relative dominance of the socio-economic groups within a particular occupation can be viewed from their population proportions as embodied in the NSS given below.

Distribution of Persons by Socio-Economic Groups

(*Percentage*)

	ST	SC	NON-SC/ST	Total
I. Rural				
1.SENA	5.0	18.3	76.7	100.0
2. AL	14.0	36.9	49.1	100.0
3. OL	14.2	29.2	56.6	100.0
4. SEA	10.7	11.3	78.0	100.0
5. OHH	7.7	16.3	76.0	100.0
6. ALL	10.8	21.1	68.1	100.0
II. Urban				
1. SE	2.3	9.5	88.2	100.0
2. RW&SE	3.6	13.6	82.8	100.0
3. CL	4.9	28.4	66.7	100.0
4. OHH	4.8	12.0	83.2	100.0
5. ALL	3.4	13.9	82.7	100.0

The Scheduled Castes have a higher representation in poorer occupation groups, such as Agricultural Labourers in rural areas and Casual Labourers in urban areas. In rural areas, the Scheduled Tribes are underrepresented in SENA and the Scheduled Castes in

SEA. The Scheduled Tribes constitute a microscopic proportion of urban population. The occupation-specific distribution of persons for each socio-economic group given below clearly demonstrates that the relative deprivation of the Scheduled Castes and Scheduled Tribes lies in their occupation.

Distribution of Persons by Occupation Groups

(Percentage)

	ST	SC	NON-SC/ST	ALL
I. Rural				
1.SENA	5.8	10.9	14.2	12.6
2. AL	35.6	48.3	19.9	27.6
3. OL	9.6	10.1	6.1	7.3
4. SEA	41.0	22.0	47.2	41.2
5. OHH	8.0	8.7	12.6	11.3
6. ALL	100.0	100.0	100.0	100.0
II. Urban				
1. SE	25.0	25.4	39.5	37.1
2. RW&SE	46.0	41.9	42.8	42.7
3. CL	18.8	26.4	10.4	12.9
4. OHH	10.2	6.3	7.3	7.3
5. ALL	100.0	100.0	100.0	100.0

About half (48.3%) of the Scheduled Castes work as Agricultural Labourers as against one-fifth (19.9%) of others, i.e., non-SC/ST. One-fifth of the Scheduled Castes (22%) are Self-Employed in Agriculture (SEA) as against nearly half (47.2%) of others. Partly as a result of the community ownership of the tribal land, the percentage of people engaged as SEA among the Scheduled Tribes (41%) is relatively higher; it is close to that among the non-ST population (41.2%). That tribal lands are not exposed to modern methods of farming is altogether a different issue.

Consumption

The per capita consumption by occupation and socio-economic groups is given below.

Consumption by Occupation and Socio-Economic Groups

(Rs. per capita per month)

	ST	SC	Others	ALL
I. Rural				
1.SENA	264.94	260.02	305.55	295.24
2. AL	202.03	209.61	227.64	217.41
3. OL	230.42	248.14	285.44	266.74
4. SEA	249.33	270.11	323.03	302.01
5. ALL	234.36	238.91	302.08	281.43
II.Urban				
1. SE	347.36	318.11	450.18	427.96
2. RW&SE	435.57	417.79	557.97	531.68
3. CL	259.25	261.28	288.36	276.99
4. ALL	330.54	342.18	480.28	458.04

In rural areas, the per capita consumption of non-SC/ST population engaged in other occupation is 70% more than that of agricultural labourers belonging to ST. In urban areas, the per capita consumption of non-SC/ST population engaged as Regular Wage and Salary Earners is more than double of that of Casual Labourers belonging to SC and ST. Generally, the difference in per capita consumption between Self-Employed in Agriculture and Agricultural Labourers and between Casual Labourers and Regular Wage and Salary Earners is sharp. More than the socio-economic group, occupation determines the level of per capita consumption.

Deviation of Consumption *(Percentage)*

	ST	SC	Others	ALL
I. Rural				
1. SENA	13.0	8.8	1.1	4.9
2. AL	-13.8	-12.3	-24.6	-22.7
3. OL	-1.7	3.9	-5.5	-5.2
4. SEA	6.4	13.1	6.9	9.8
II Urban				
1. SE	-8.7	-7.0	-6.3	-5.0
2.RW&SE	14.5	22.1	16.2	16.7
3. CL	-31.9	-23.6	-40.0	-39.0

N.B.: Deviation is measured from the respective national average.

Inter-occupation disparity in per capita consumption within each socio-economic group given above shows that for all population, the per capita consumption of AL and CL are less than their respective national averages by 22.7% and 39.0% respectively, whereas that of SEA and RW&SE are more than the national averages by 9.8% and 16.7% respectively.

The disparity in per capita consumption is also viewed for some of the food items such as, milk and milk products, meat, fish, eggs and fruits which have shown phenomenal growth in the past few years, besides, clothing and durable goods. The table below gives the consumption index of these items setting the average of all occupations as 100. SEA spend about two to three times on these items as compared to Agricultural Labourers and Casual Labourers. Such differences are not pronounced in the case of items of basic necessities.

Consumption Index

(*All Population*=100)

	Milk and Products	Meat Fish and Egg	Fruits	Beverages	Clothing	Durable Goods
I. Rural						
1 SENA	94	126	120	120	100	120
2. AL	44	80	58	77	64	46
3. OL	68	112	96	131	80	107
4. SEA	138	91	102	82	122	123
II. Urban						
1. SE	106	95	102	82	89	78
2. RW&SE	111	120	117	118	122	145
3. CL	38	77	47	63	48	25

Poverty

The incidence of poverty by occupation and socio-economic groups is estimated from the respective consumption distribution of the NSS and the poverty line of the area. The percentage of very poor, poor and upper group of non-poor, estimated for each of these occupation and socio-economic groups in rural areas is given below.

Poverty by Occupation and Socio-Economic Groups in Rural Areas

(Percentage)

	ST	SC	SC&ST	NON-SC/ST	ALL
I. Poverty Ratio					
1. SENA	44.7	38.2	39.6	29.5	32.2
2. AL	63.9	60.0	61.1	52.3	56.8
3. OL	51.7	41.5	44.8	35.6	39.7
4. SEA	47.1	37.7	42.3	25.6	29.2
5. ALL	52.0	48.3	49.5	31.3	37.2
II. Very Poor					
1. SENA	21.6	14.3	15.9	10.0	11.1
2. AL	33.3	29.9	30.9	23.9	27.2
3. OL	18.3	15.7	16.6	12.7	14.6
4. SEA	21.4	14.0	17.6	7.9	10.0
5. ALL	24.8	21.8	22.8	11.5	15.3
III. Upper Non-Poor					
1. SENA	23.2	23.1	23.1	35.0	31.7
2. AL	11.2	11.3	11.3	15.5	13.2
3. OL	16.2	20.0	18.8	28.6	24.2
4. SEA	18.1	23.2	20.7	37.1	33.2
5. ALL	16.5	18.0	17.8	33.5	28.6

About 60% of the Agricultural Labourers belonging to Scheduled Castes and Scheduled Tribes are poor; half of them being very poor. The preponderance of SC/STs among the Agricultural Labourers distinguishes them from other occupations and classes. For example, if rural India consisted of 1000 persons, 319 of them would be SCs and STs and 141 of them Agricultural Labourers. But among the 681persons categorised as "others", i.e, non-SC/ST the number of Agricultural Labourers would have been only 135. It is this difference that makes poverty harsh on the SCs and STs. The caste based difference in poverty ratio also surfaces from the average rates obtained among the Self-Employed, in which the difference between the SC/STs and "others" is substantial.

Poverty by Occupation and Socio-Economic Groups in Urban Areas

(Percentage)

	ST	SC	SC&ST	NON-SC/ST	ALL
I. Poverty Ratio					
1. SE	51.3	53.2	52.9	32.3	36.2
2. RW&SE	28.5	33.8	32.7	18.0	20.9
3. CL	64.6	67.7	67.2	58.9	62.6
4. ALL	40.7	49.8	46.9	28.4	32.3
II. Very Poor					
1. SE	24.9	28.2	27.5	13.7	15.8
2. RW&SE	13.3	13.9	13.8	6.2	7.3
3. CL	36.6	40.4	39.9	32.0	35.8
4. ALL	20.1	25.7	24.3	12.3	14.9
III. Upper Non-Poor					
1. SE	26.0	17.7	19.3	37.9	34.1
2. RW&SE	37.1	32.4	33.4	53.5	49.8
3. CL	7.9	8.9	8.8	13.9	11.5
4. ALL	29.1	21.2	23.4	42.9	38.9

In urban areas, the poverty ratio as well as the percentage of very poor among the Self-Employeds belonging to SC/STs are much more than that among the non-SC/STs. Similar is the case among the RW&SE, though their average level of poverty is least among all the occupations. However, the percentage of Self Employed is less. To repeat in the manner the rural scene is described in the previous paragraph, if there were 1000 persons in urban India, 173 of them would be SCs and STs and 44 or one-quarter of them, would be self-employed. On the contrary, among the 827 non-SC/ST people, 354, i.e., 42.8% of them are self-employed. The crux of the matter is that the majority of "others" are engaged in an occupation, which bears a lower poverty rate. These suggest that poverty and deprivation are associated with particular occupation, which, more than the socio-economic groups is relevant for devising the strategy for anti-poverty programmes.

Gender Groups

The Directive Principles of State Policy in The Constitution of India state: "The State shall, in particular, direct its policy towards securing that the citizen, men and women equally, have the right to an adequate means of livelihood." (Article 39) The mention of equality between men and women in economic activity at that time was indeed a bold step as the socio-economic traditions were governed by deep-rooted social and cultural practices and behaviours. The prevailing social practices divorced the females from a fair share of economic rights, resulting in extreme form of privation among the female-headed families, which emerged primarily due to the absence of a male head.

India has come a long way since then. Large social and economic advances in the past half a century have re-constructed the fabric of India's social and economic life by overcoming mass poverty and raising the masses of the people from privation. The country witnessed a change with remarkable rapidity and the winds of change blown through economic growth and development engulfed not only the city dwellers but also the poorest of the poor and the downtrodden in the rural areas.

According to 1993-94 consumer expenditure survey of the NSSO, 9.7% of the rural households and 10.6% of urban households are female headed. These households are smaller in size as compared to the male headed households. The average size of female headed households is 3.2 persons in both rural and urban areas. The average size of male headed households is 5.1 persons in rural areas and 4.7 persons in urban areas. The smaller size of the female headed households can be reflection of prosperity or deprivation. A comparison of the per capita consumption and poverty indices of male and female headed households demonstrate that the role of women in the process of development has been exemplary even as the likelihood of some of them living in destitution can not be ruled out. These in rural and urban areas at national level are given in Table-3.10.

Table 3.10 : Consumption and Poverty by Gender Groups

	Male Headed House-holds	Female Headed House-holds	All House-holds
I. Rural Areas			
1.Per Capita Monthly Consumption (Rs.)			
(a) Bottom 30%	149.69	148.65	149.52
(b) Middle 40%	238.77	250.83	239.96
(c) Top 30%	465.87	511.38	468.53
(d) All Population	280.18	298.34	281.40
2.Inequality (Lorenz Ratio)	0.2802	0.3039	0.2816
3.Poverty			
(a) Very Poor	15.25	15.46	15.27
(b) Moderately Poor	22.12	20.00	21.98
(c) Poor	37.37	35.46	37.23
(d) Lower Non-Poor	34.32	32.03	34.18
(e) Upper Non-Poor	28.30	32.51	28.57
(f) Non-Poor	62.63	64.54	62.75
II. Urban Areas			
1.Per Capita Monthly Consumption (Rs.)			
(a) Bottom 30%	208.87	193.59	206.86
(b) Middle 40%	365.50	347.00	364.00
(c) Top 30%	835.00	811.08	834.48
(d) All Population	459.00	440.20	458.00
2.Inequality (Lorenz Ratio)	0.3382	0.3502	0.3400
3.Poverty			
(a) Very Poor	14.56	18.36	14.85
(b) Moderately Poor	17.34	18.51	17.43
(c) Poor	31.90	36.87	32.28
(d) Lower Non-Poor	28.96	27.37	28.85
(e) Upper Non-Poor	39.15	35.76	38.87
(f) Non-Poor	68.10	63.13	67.72

Consumption and Poverty by Gender Groups

In rural areas, the per capita consumption of female headed households is 6.5% more than that of male headed households. The per capita consumption of top 30% of the population in the female headed households is 10% more than that of male headed households. This perhaps is a sign of the emergence of women as independent entities in the process of development. In urban areas, however, the per capita consumption of female headed households is 4% less than that of male headed households. The inequality in consumption distribution among the female headed households is higher than that in male headed households in both rural and urban areas. And, inequality in urban areas is higher than in rural areas, a phenomenon that is evident for the entire population.

In rural areas, the poverty ratio among male headed households (37.4%) is more than that in female headed households (35.5%). The reverse is the case in urban areas, where the poverty ratio among the female headed households (36.9%) is more than that in male headed households (31.9%). The percentage of very poor in male and female headed households does not differ in rural areas but in urban areas it is slightly more in female headed households.

Religion Groups

A particular system of faith and worship may not influence the levels of living but it is worthwhile to check it with the help of the numeric and study the pattern of consumption and poverty across the religion groups. The NSS consumer expenditure data is not stratified by religion groups. Since the sample proportions of two major religion groups, the Hindus and the Muslims, are found to be close to their respective population proportion as per the 1991 census, liberty has been taken to use this data to estimate per capita consumption and poverty indices by religion groups, such as, Hindu, Muslim, Christian, Sikh, Jain and Buddhist. These are given in Table 3.11 and for the reasons mentioned above, may be treated as merely indicative.

Table 3.11 : Consumption and Poverty by Religion Groups

	Hindu	Muslim	Christian	Sikh	Jain	Buddhist
1	2	3	4	5	6	7
I. Rural Areas						
1.Per Capita Monthly Consumption (Rs.)						
(a) Bottom 30%	132.77	135.27	141.29	236.05	206.56	84.06
(b) Middle 40%	238.32	228.64	271.47	372.24	360.46	196.75
(c) Top 30%	478.09	450.03	600.64	727.75	616.85	399.19
(d) All Population	278.59	267.05	331.17	438.04	391.21	223.67
2.Inequality	0.2788	0.2698	0.3179	0.2654	0.2490	0.2568
(Lorenz Ratio)						
3.Poverty						
(a) Very Poor	15.34	15.31	12.85	1.28	3.93	28.55
(b) Moderately Poor	22.16	25.97	17.40	4.66	10.07	26.79
(c) Poor	37.50	41.27	30.25	5.94	14.01	55.34
(d) Lower Non-Poor	34.84	35.40	29.82	27.99	16.20	27.51
(e) Upper Non-Poor	27.66	23.33	39.93	66.07	69.79	17.15
(f) Non-Poor	62.50	58.73	69.75	94.06	85.99	44.66

(Contd.)

Table 3.11 *(Contd.)*

1	2	3	4	5	6	7
II. Urban Areas						
1.Per Capita Monthly Consumption (Rs.)						
(a) Bottom 30%	194.06	143.60	326.58	283.90	372.94	120.78
(b) Middle 40%	377.24	290.65	442.39	507.12	603.46	320.04
(c) Top 30%	866.94	632.60	1004.07	1449.05	1134.29	700.76
(d) All Population	469.20	349.12	576.15	722.73	693.55	374.48
2.Inequality	0.3355	0.2969	0.3390	0.4123	0.2712	0.3133
(Lorenz Ratio)						
3.Poverty						
(a) Very Poor	13.03	23.94	9.97	3.99	0.44	26.31
(b) Moderately Poor	17.28	25.30	11.37	8.88	4.93	17.71
(c) Poor	30.31	49.23	21.34	12.88	5.37	44.01
(d) Lower Non-Poor	28.92	28.76	26.35	27.24	12.78	27.56
(e) Upper Non-Poor	40.77	22.01	52.32	59.89	81.85	28.43
(f) Non-Poor	69.69	50.77	78.66	87.12	94.63	55.99

Consumption and Poverty by Religion Groups

In rural areas, the per capita consumption of the Sikhs is one and a half times of the national average. The impact of increased agricultural income is evident enough. The per capita consumption of the Hindus is 4% higher than the Muslims and marginally less than the national average. The disparity in per capita consumption between Hindus and Muslims is not evident in rural areas, but gets surfaced in urban areas, where the per capita consumption of Hindus exceeds that of Muslims by one-third. High consumption among the religion groups is accompanied by high inequality and *vice-versa*.

In rural areas, the poverty ratio among the Muslims (41.3%) is greater the Hindus (37.5%). But, the percentage of very poor (15%) and moderately rich (35%) is identical for Hindus and Muslims. The poverty ratio among the Christians is relatively low but their percentage of very poor are almost similar to Hindus and Muslims. High per capita consumption nearly frees the Sikhs (5.9%) from poverty. Low per capita consumption and low inequality produces poverty ratio among the Buddhists (55.3%), which is about one and a half times of the national rural poverty ratio (37.2%). Buddhists include neo-Buddhists, which is the religion of many Scheduled Castes.

Hindu-Muslim disparity in the incidence of poverty, which is virtually missing in rural areas, is pronounced in urban. As against the national urban poverty ratio of 32.3%, the poverty ratio is 33.0% among the Hindus and 49.2% among the Muslims.

Household Size

The size of a household has important bearing on levels of living. Per capita consumption and poverty among the households, classified by their sizes bring out the economic rationale of small-family norm. Per capita consumption and poverty of households of sizes ranging from one to six and above in rural and urban areas at national level are given in Table-3.12.

Consumption and Poverty by Household Size

Per capita consumptio is observed to be inversely related with

Table 3.12 : Consumption and Poverty by Household size

	Single Member House-hold	Two Member House-hold	Three Member House-hold	Four Member House-hold	Five Member House-hold	Household with Six and more Members
1	2	3	4	5	6	7
I. Rural						
1.Per Capita Monthly Consumption (Rs.)						
(a) Bottom 30%	191.05	186.66	174.47	162.21	151.72	143.17
(b) Middle 40%	353.20	307.46	279.78	260.63	240.88	222.92
(c) Top 30%	798.14	599.89	552.09	527.42	467.34	412.94
(d) All	438.04	358.95	329.88	311.14	282.07	256.00
2.Inequality (Lorenz Ratio)	0.3238	0.2847	0.2820	0.2939	0.2781	0.2636
3.Poverty						
(a) Very Poor	6.42	6.34	8.44	11.27	14.45	18.63
(b) Moderately Poor	10.45	12.52	15.46	18.98	21.85	24.83
(c) Poor	16.87	18.85	23.90	30.26	36.31	43.46
(d) Lower Non-Poor	25.02	33.06	35.16	35.43	35.24	33.55
(e) Upper Non-Poor	58.11	48.09	40.94	34.31	28.46	22.99
(f) Non-Poor	83.13	81.15	76.10	69.74	63.69	56.54

(Contd.)

Table 3.12 *(Contd.)*

1	2	3	4	5	6	7
II. Urban						
1.Per Capita Monthly Consumption (Rs.)						
(a) Bottom 30%	314.59	277.94	266.93	247.70	218.97	186.04
(b) Middle 40%	678.70	530.77	489.80	439.61	374.89	307.98
(c) Top 30%	1366.14	1255.50	1111.70	956.88	787.12	627.42
(d) All	775.70	672.34	609.51	537.22	451.78	367.23
2.Inequality (Lorenz Ratio)	0.3230	0.3600	0.3421	0.3239	0.3115	0.3016
3.Poverty						
(a) Very Poor	6.42	5.31	5.74	7.79	12.30	21.56
(b) Moderately Poor	4.98	9.70	10.57	13.19	16.49	22.05
(c) Poor	11.40	15.01	16.31	20.98	28.79	43.60
(d) Lower Non-Poor	11.30	21.51	25.82	27.65	30.67	30.65
(e) Upper Non-Poor	77.30	63.47	57.87	51.37	40.54	25.74
(f) Non-Poor	88.60	84.99	83.69	79.02	71.21	56.40

household size. The relation is stronger in urban areas as compared to rural, and in the top expenditure brackets as compared to the bottom. The per capita consumption of single member households is 71% higher than that of six-member households in rural areas and 2.1 times in urban. The per capita consumption of a conventional small family of three members, a couple and a child exceeds that of the families with six and more members by 29% in rural areas and 66% in urban areas.

There is a perfect negative association between inequality in consumption distribution and household size in rural areas. The inequality is highest among the single member households and lowest among the households with six and more of family members, and the inequality declines in an almost secular fashion as the household size increases. The behaviour of inequality in urban areas is observed to be different. It is high in two member and three member households and somewhat low in the households with five or six members.

Poverty ratio and household size are positively associated. In rural areas, the poverty ratio among the six member households (43.5%) is two and a half times of the single member households (16.9%) and about twice of the three member households (23.9%). In urban areas, the poverty ratio of six member households (43.6%) is nearly four times of single member households (11.4%) and two and a half times of three member households (16.3%). Among the smaller households, the percentage of very poor is low and the upper group of non-poor is high.

Land and Rural Poverty

The equality in land ownership is a policy essential for economic development as land possession has a profound impact on consumption and the levels of living in rural areas. The data on land possession of households have been collected in the consumer expenditure survey by ascertaining the area of land "owned", "leased in," "neither owned nor leased in" and "leased out" by the households. The land possessed by the household is arrived at by subtracting the area of land "leased out" from the sum of the first three. The

Table 3.13 : Conspumtion and Inequality by Land Possession

S. No.	Land Possession (Hectare/Family)	Percent-age of Persons	Per capita Consumption (Rs./Month)	Inequality (Lorenz Ratio)
0	1	2	3	4
1.	No Land	10.29	262.49	0.2879
2.	0.01 - 0.40	36.54	266.85	0.2837
3.	0.40 - 1.00	19.20	269.25	0.2600
4.	1.00 - 2.00	15.94	284.54	0.2671
5.	2.00 - 3.00	7.36	306.77	0.2765
6.	3.00 - 4.00	3.53	316.85	0.2681
7.	4.00 - 5.00	2.49	353.53	0.3155
8.	> 5.00	4.66	371.07	0.2894

land "neither owned nor leased in" is the land for which the household takes title of ownership without transacting a lease agreement. The distribution of persons by size of land possession so obtained is given in Table-3.13. This may not provide a clear picture of land distribution because of its connectivity with household consumption expenditure survey. Nevertheless, it gives an idea about the level of living that follows with certain quantity of land possession among rural families. The land distribution pattern as emerged from the survey shows that among the rural households:

(a) 10.3% do not posses land at all.
(b) 55.7% possess less than one hectare of land.
(c) 15.9% possess between one and two hectares of land.
(d) 10.9% possess between two and four hectares of land.

The households in (b) can be equated with marginal farmers, (c) with small farmers and (d) as semi-medium farmers. The nexus between per capita consumption and land possession is observed as:

(a) Per capita consumption with different sizes of land possession up to one hectare per family is almost similar.

(b) Per capita consumption rises when the land possession per family exceeds one hectare.

(c) With more than five hectares of land in the family, the per capita consumption becomes 35% more than those with one to three hectares of land.

The message in its transparent form is that less than a hectare of land per family is not sufficient to raise consumption and hence the impoverishment of the marginal farmers. The disparity in per capita consumption consequent upon land possession is not observed in lower expenditure groups. The nexus between land possession and inequality in consumption distribution (Lorenz Ratio) is observed as:

(a) Lorenz ratio is less than the national average for families possessing 0.4 to 2.0 hectares of land.

(b) Lorenz ratio increases as land possession rises; it is maximum for families possessing 4.0 to 5.0 hectares of land.

The poverty ratio among the families classified by their land possession, given in Table-3.14 demonstrates its electrifying effect on rural poverty. The poverty ratio of the persons without land and up to 0.40 hectares of land is above the national rural poverty ratio (37.2%). The poverty ratio declines sharply as land possession rises from one hectare. The poverty ratio is:

(a) 34% for persons with 1 to 2 hectares of land,

(b) 29% for persons with 2 to 3 hectares of land,

(c) 25% for persons with 3 to 5 hectares, and

(d) 18% for persons when the land possession exceeds 5 hectares.

Land possession impacts greatly the very poor. However, there are persons below the poverty line possessing 4 to 5 hectares of land. Land alone does not guarantee a rise in consumption and improvement in level of living. It brings into surface the role of inputs and infrastructure. Generally, land availability has been

Table 3.14 : Land Possession and Poverty

S.No.	Land Possession (Hectors/Family)	Very Poor	Moderately Poor	Poor	Lower Non-Poor	Upper Non-Poor	Non-Poor
0	1	2	3	4	5	6	7
1.	No Land	20.58	23.12	43.70	30.94	25.35	56.30
2.	0.01 - 0.40	18.41	24.31	42.73	32.83	24.45	57.27
3.	0.40 - 1.00	14.60	23.23	37.83	36.53	25.64	62.17
4.	1.00 - 2.00	12.78	21.18	33.96	36.74	29.31	66.04
5.	2.00 - 3.00	10.99	18.06	29.05	34.88	36.07	70.95
6.	3.00 - 4.00	9.02	15.89	24.91	35.25	39.84	75.09
7.	4.00 - 5.00	7.68	15.93	23.61	34.75	41.64	76.39
8.	> 5.00	5.59	12.55	18.14	31.38	50.48	81.86

Table 3.15 : State-wise Distribution of Persons by Land Possession

(Percentage)

S.No.	States	No Land	0.01-0.4	0.4-1.0	1.0-2.0	2.0-4.0	4+
0	1	2	3	4	5	6	7
1.	Andhra Pradesh	9.02	43.01	19.82	12.94	9.47	5.75
2.	Assam	1.44	41.84	22.14	24.68	8.25	1.66
3.	Bihar	7.73	46.16	19.70	16.34	7.25	2.82
4.	Gujarat	19.64	28.55	15.68	14.87	11.99	9.26
5.	Haryana	3.14	46.93	8.33	12.42	15.57	13.60
6.	Himachal Pradesh	4.16	33.92	33.26	17.72	8.10	2.84
7.	Karnataka	13.98	26.02	18.52	16.96	13.36	11.16
8.	Kerala	1.74	76.95	13.83	5.28	1.52	0.67
9.	Madhya Pradesh	10.96	14.69	15.04	20.84	21.61	16.86
10.	Maharashtra	23.12	19.89	14.78	16.20	14.14	11.86
11.	Orissa	6.07	38.15	24.95	18.34	9.92	2.57
12.	Punjab	25.34	35.02	6.88	10.29	10.59	11.88
13.	Rajasthan	4.24	16.72	18.11	18.24	19.56	23.14
14.	Tamil Nadu	16.86	52.48	15.58	9.05	4.26	1.77
15.	Uttar Pradesh	5.68	34.61	24.67	18.96	11.14	4.94
16.	West Bengal	11.06	51.43	21.14	10.80	4.70	0.88
17.	All India	10.29	36.54	19.20	15.94	10.88	7.15

instrumental in raising the consumption of non-poor, particularly, the upper-group, proportionately more than the poor.

The state-wise distribution of persons by land possession is given in Table-3.15. The percentage of landless labourers is high (20 to 25%) in Gujarat, Maharashtra and Punjab, though, may be for disparate reasons. Small farmers almost entirely predominate Kerala and to a great extent Tamil Nadu and West Bengal. In Kerala, the land size of as much as 77% of the persons is less than 0.40 hectare. Similar are the land sizes for more than 50% of the persons in Tamil Nadu and West Bengal. The decline in rural poverty in these states has been significant. Between 1973-74 and 1993-94, the rural poverty ratio declined from 59.2% to 25.8% in Kerala, from 57.4% to 32.5% in Tamil Nadu and from 73.2% to 40.8% in West Bengal. The nexus is worth noting.

State-wise percentage of persons below the poverty line for types of land holdings is given in Table-3.16. It indicates the favourable impact of land availability on rural poverty. The poverty ratio among the class of landholders in the states is similar to that obtained at the national level. There is inter-state variation in the pattern, of course.

The impact of land availability on rural poverty is such that the poverty ratio among the small and marginal farmers (less than one hectare per family) with the exception of Madhya Pradesh, Maharashtra, Orissa and Rajasthan, is about twice of that among the semi-medium farmers (two to four hectares per family). The poverty ratio among the landless labourers and marginal farmers are significantly higher in Assam and Bihar. In some states, the poverty ratio among the landless is less than those with marginal land (less than 0.4 hectares). Perhaps, the impact of wage-employment on poverty is felt.

Two issues surface from the state-wise estimate of poverty by land possession. First, land availability does not produce identical impact on poverty ratio in the states. Secondly, and partly as an impact of the first, the inter-state disparity in the poverty ratio increases with land availability.

Table 3.16 : State-wise Poverty Ratio by Land Possession

S.No.	States	No Land	0.01-0.4	0.4 -1.0	1.0-2.0	2.0-4.0	4+
0	1	2	3	4	5	6	7
1.	Andhra Pradesh	17.19	17.80	15.14	13.97	13.98	7.67
2.	Assam	68.90	55.68	42.89	35.37	25.13	10.14
3.	Bihar	68.32	67.98	52.99	50.02	31.73	26.13
4.	Gujarat	26.50	24.00	28.79	23.22	12.66	6.71
5.	Haryana	34.43	37.63	20.66	21.86	22.78	8.04
6.	Himachal Pradesh	22.57	33.49	32.71	23.82	26.49	19.44
7.	Karnataka	43.73	30.33	28.12	30.72	21.37	23.31
8.	Kerala	14.28	29.32	13.92	8.80	8.24	8.70
9.	Madhya Pradesh	48.88	52.54	48.27	42.03	35.90	23.35
10.	Maharashtra	50.18	35.52	35.60	35.10	36.55	26.35
11.	Orissa	44.20	56.78	52.56	45.30	36.44	20.70
12.	Punjab	19.48	16.36	6.48	3.76	1.81	0.10
13.	Rajasthan	32.65	33.32	35.43	28.21	23.03	14.36
14.	Tamil Nadu	30.04	36.87	32.54	23.70	16.91	7.60
15.	Uttar Pradesh	51.73	51.63	42.79	36.32	26.25	22.21
16.	West Bengal	50.81	48.41	34.11	21.95	13.38	13.29
17.	All India	43.70	42.73	37.83	33.96	27.71	20.04

Table 3.17 : Distribution of Persons by Land Possession in Occupation and Socio Economic Groups

(Hectares per Family)

S.No.	States	No Land	0.01-0.4	0.4-1.0	1.0-2.0	2.0-4.0	4+
0	1	2	3	4	5	6	7
I. Occupation							
1	SENA	15.6	59.8	14.2	6.3	3.0	1.1
2	AL	17.6	57.9	16.5	6.1	1.6	0.3
3	OL	18.7	59.3	13.8	5.6	1.8	0.8
4	SEA	0.6	8.9	24.6	28.5	22.1	15.3
II. Socio-Economic Groups							
1	ST	10.7	26.4	21.7	20.6	14.3	6.3
2	SC	16.5	49.7	16.8	9.8	5.0	2.2

N.B.: Legends in Table 3.1.

Table 3.18 : Poverty Ratio by Land Possession in Occupation and Socio Economic Groups

(Hectares per Family)

S.No.	States	No Land	0.01-0.4	0.4-1.0	1.0-2.0	2.0-4.0	4+
0	1	2	3	4	5	6	7
I. Occupation							
1	SENA	33.9	33.2	29.0	30.9	20.2	11.9
2	AL	56.4	56.6	57.3	58.3	56.8	55.2
3	OL	38.8	38.8	41.6	44.4	41.8	39.5
4	SEA	40.9	35.0	33.2	31.2	26.6	19.2
II. Socio-Economic Groups							
1	ST	54.0	54.3	53.9	50.8	51.3	40.1
2	SC	50.0	50.6	47.3	43.5	36.7	36.9

N.B.: Legends in Table 3.1.

Land Possession by Occupation

Table-3.17 gives the percentage of persons by land possession in occupation and socio-economic groups. The percentage of marginal farmers is high among the SENA, AL and OL and low among the SEA. It is also high among the Scheduled Castes but not among the Scheduled Tribes.

The poverty ratio by land possession among the occupation and socio-economic groups given in Table-3.18 highlights the significance of the occupation structure in rural areas. Land possession does not influence the poverty ratio of some occupation groups. The poverty ratio among the Agricultural Labourers, who by far are the poorest, is not sensitive to land possession while that among SENA and SEA declines sharply with increase in land possession. The poverty ratio among the persons possessing more than 4 hectares of land is 55.2% among the Agricultural Labourers as compared to 19.2% among the SENA and only 11.9% among the SEA. However, there is evidence of decline in the poverty ratio among the Scheduled Castes and Scheduled Tribes with increase in their land possession.

4

CONSUMPTION AND INEQUALITY AT REGIONAL LEVEL

Per capita consumption is treated as the prime indicator of level of living in a low-income developing economy. India is no exception. In effect, the use of consumption data for such purposes is extensive in India partly because of absence of income data and partly because of regular availability of consumption data from Government agencies. The consumer expenditure data collected by the National Sample Survey Organisation in its 50th Round (July, 1993 to June, 1994) from 115 thousand 350 families (60% of these families are drawn from rural areas and 40% from urban areas) has been used to assess the levels of living at state and sub-state level. The sub-state levels are the NSS regions formed by grouping contiguous districts, similar in density of population and cropping pattern. The entire country is divided into 78 NSS regions, of which the data of 59 regions, spread over 16 states, have been used here. These 59 regions contain 97% of the rural and 93% of the urban population in the country. The mapping of districts and NSS regions (prevailing in 1993-94) and the population proportion of the NSS regions are appended at the end for reference (Appendix-II and III).

Consumption

Region-wise per capita consumption of different fractiles of the population and the inequality in its distribution, measured by Lorenz

Table 4.1 : Consumption and Inequality in Rural Regions

S.No.	State/Region	Share of Consumption (%) Bottom 30%	Top 30%	Top 30%/ Bottom 30%	Per Capita Consumption (Rs./month) Bottom 30%	Top 30%	All	Lorenz Ratio
0	1	2	3	4	5	6	7	8
ANDHRA PRADESH		14.88	51.67	3.47	143.20	497.24	288.70	0.2854
1	Coastal	14.99	50.99	3.40	138.79	472.12	277.77	0.2769
2	Inland Northern	15.29	51.02	3.34	151.09	504.16	296.45	0.2795
3	South Western	12.66	56.29	4.45	123.81	550.50	293.39	0.3370
4	Inland Southern	15.52	50.97	3.28	158.52	520.59	306.41	0.2870
ASSAM		19.93	42.25	2.12	171.47	363.50	258.11	0.1763
5	Plains Eastern	19.96	42.22	2.12	179.83	380.39	270.29	0.1765
6	Plains Western	20.00	42.41	2.12	166.85	353.81	250.28	0.1753
7	Hills	22.07	40.49	1.83	194.26	356.39	264.06	0.1512
BIHAR		14.92	48.78	3.27	108.57	354.96	218.30	0.2224
8	Southern	14.47	50.30	3.48	103.49	359.75	214.56	0.2315
9	Northern	14.99	48.31	3.22	107.55	346.61	215.24	0.2157
10	Central	15.38	48.15	3.13	115.74	362.36	225.77	0.2236
GUJARAT		17.11	46.63	2.73	172.99	471.46	303.32	0.2358
11	Eastern	17.16	44.34	2.58	161.41	417.06	282.18	0.2134
12	Plains Northern	17.08	46.99	2.75	174.94	481.30	307.28	0.2379

(Contd.)

Table 4.1 *(Contd.)*

0	1	2	3	4	5	6	7	8
13	Plains Southern	15.56	50.61	3.25	155.98	507.35	300.74	0.2709
14	Dry Areas	17.04	47.16	2.77	166.53	460.89	293.19	0.2375
15	Saurashtra	18.72	45.39	2.42	203.80	494.16	326.61	0.2210
HARYANA		14.49	52.07	3.59	185.96	668.25	385.01	0.3009
16	Eastern	15.30	50.51	3.30	178.10	587.97	349.22	0.2791
17	Western	13.93	53.67	3.85	203.05	782.33	437.30	0.3160
18	Himachal Pradesh	15.92	50.05	3.14	186.07	584.97	350.63	0.2763
KARNATAKA		14.53	50.61	3.48	130.47	454.46	269.39	0.2666
19	Coastal and Ghat	16.83	49.30	2.93	206.96	606.24	368.91	0.2704
20	Inland Eastern	17.63	47.02	2.67	175.84	468.96	299.21	0.2355
21	Inland Southern	15.65	49.19	3.14	137.97	433.64	264.47	0.2536
22	Inland Northern	13.54	51.63	3.81	111.53	425.29	247.12	0.2631
KERALA		15.02	50.74	3.38	195.47	660.31	390.41	0.2879
23	Northern	15.34	49.75	3.24	183.36	594.68	358.60	0.2792
24	Southern	14.92	51.23	3.43	204.69	702.84	411.58	0.2885
MADHYA PRADESH		13.41	52.41	3.91	112.65	440.26	252.01	0.2769
25	Chattisgarh	17.08	46.93	2.75	129.40	355.56	227.29	0.2149
26	Vindhya	15.29	49.52	3.24	128.49	416.15	252.11	0.2467
27	Central	14.43	49.39	3.42	103.19	353.20	214.54	0.2304
28	Malwa	15.55	48.51	3.12	147.56	460.34	284.69	0.2516

(Contd.)

Table 4.1 *(Contd.)*

0	1	2	3	4	5	6	7	8
29	South	10.61	59.48	5.61	95.90	537.64	271.17	0.3640
30	South Western	-	-	-	-	-	185.35	0.2862
31	Northern	15.25	49.34	3.24	170.70	552.30	335.81	0.2687
MAHARASHTRA		12.50	54.08	4.33	113.61	491.52	272.66	0.3024
32	Coastal	15.71	50.78	3.23	189.53	612.61	361.92	0.2841
33	Inland Western	15.45	49.47	3.20	153.71	492.18	298.47	0.2651
34	Inland Northern	13.81	51.17	3.71	107.14	396.99	232.75	0.2571
35	Inland Central	5.64	64.02	11.35	49.29	559.53	262.20	0.3777
36	Inland Eastern	14.12	51.89	3.67	108.72	399.54	230.99	0.2609
37	Eastern	15.39	49.76	3.23	117.93	381.29	229.88	0.2462
ORISSA		13.52	51.24	3.79	99.07	375.47	219.83	0.2433
38	Coastal	14.64	49.83	3.40	110.57	376.33	226.57	0.2377
39	Southern	9.81	53.37	5.44	58.61	318.85	179.23	0.2121
40	Northern	13.72	51.02	3.72	106.15	394.74	232.11	0.2499
PUNJAB		16.53	49.84	3.02	238.58	719.36	433.00	0.2646
41	Northern	16.93	49.51	2.92	253.10	740.16	448.49	0.2576
42	Southern	16.05	49.90	3.11	220.81	686.51	412.73	0.2719
RAJASTHAN		16.18	48.79	3.02	173.88	524.31	322.39	0.2598
43	Western	17.95	45.82	2.55	183.59	468.63	306.83	0.2261
44	North Eastern	17.23	45.92	2.67	196.65	524.08	342.39	0.2324

(Contd.)

Table 4.1 *(Contd.)*

0	1	2	3	4	5	6	7	8
45	Southern	14.90	54.32	3.65	145.54	530.60	293.04	0.3289
46	South Eastern	13.09	54.13	4.14	143.94	595.21	329.88	0.3100
TAMIL NADU		13.43	53.81	4.01	131.44	526.66	293.62	0.3069
47	Coastal Northern	11.28	58.85	5.22	107.87	562.76	286.88	0.3535
48	Coastal	15.53	50.52	3.25	169.58	551.64	327.58	0.2832
49	Southern	13.93	50.56	3.63	119.75	434.63	257.89	0.2616
50	Inland	15.61	51.33	3.29	164.54	541.05	316.22	0.2862
UTTAR PRADESH		14.11	51.64	3.66	128.79	471.35	273.83	0.2782
51	Himalayan	17.64	47.38	2.69	180.09	483.70	306.27	0.2402
52	Western	15.40	50.29	3.27	162.82	531.72	317.19	0.2738
53	Central	12.25	53.48	4.37	102.68	448.29	251.47	0.2829
54	Eastern	14.76	50.35	3.41	122.87	419.13	249.73	0.2587
55	Southern	9.29	57.96	6.24	68.15	425.21	220.09	0.2983
WEST BENGAL		16.75	48.58	2.90	155.65	451.44	278.78	0.2509
56	Himalayan	20.67	41.12	1.99	149.59	297.59	217.11	0.1497
57	Eastern Plains	15.74	50.57	3.21	142.93	459.23	272.43	0.2756
58	Central Plains	16.34	47.70	2.92	163.61	477.62	300.39	0.2463
59	Western Plains	18.04	47.34	2.62	167.95	440.74	279.30	0.2345
	All India	15.94	49.95	3.13	149.52	468.53	281.40	0.2816

Table 4.2 : Consumption and Inequality in Urban Regions

S.No.	State/Region	Share of Consumption (%) Bottom 30%	Top 30%	Top 30%/ Bottom 30%	Per Capita Consumption (Rs./month) Bottom 30%	Top 30%	All	Lorenz Ratio
0	1	2	3	4	5	6	7	8
ANDHRA PRADESH		12.68	54.85	4.33	172.73	747.17	408.66	0.3200
1	Coastal	12.56	55.32	4.40	159.79	703.78	381.66	0.3149
2	Inland Northern	13.27	54.17	4.08	203.61	831.18	460.32	0.3209
3	South Western	11.64	54.49	4.68	148.26	694.06	382.12	0.3068
4	Inland Southern	12.57	53.97	4.29	150.72	647.12	359.71	0.2985
ASSAM		15.46	51.22	3.31	236.32	782.93	458.57	0.2862
5	Plains Eastern	15.72	50.27	3.20	263.41	842.36	502.70	0.2818
6	Plains Western	15.26	51.68	3.39	219.23	742.45	430.99	0.2884
7	Hills	18.51	43.32	2.34	271.26	634.84	439.64	0.1918
BIHAR		11.45	55.75	4.87	134.74	656.05	353.03	0.3065
8	Southern	12.64	55.33	4.38	172.78	756.34	410.09	0.3218
9	Northern	9.16	57.23	6.25	87.81	548.64	287.60	0.2795
10	Central	11.85	53.15	4.49	129.70	581.73	328.35	0.2729
GUJARAT		15.07	51.05	3.39	228.15	772.86	454.18	0.2871
11	Eastern	16.87	50.43	2.99	228.93	684.35	407.11	0.2675
12	Plains Northern	14.70	50.81	3.46	227.17	785.22	463.62	0.2892

(*Contd.*)

Table 4.2 *(Contd.)*

0	1	2	3	4	5	6	7	8
13	Plains Southern	14.38	51.27	3.57	245.23	874.34	511.61	0.3000
14	Dry Areas	11.72	56.92	4.86	220.07	1068.82	563.33	0.3503
15	Saurashtra	17.97	45.72	2.54	226.61	576.56	378.32	0.2177
HARYANA		15.00	50.24	3.35	236.96	793.66	473.92	0.2802
16	Eastern	15.30	49.69	3.25	234.80	762.56	460.39	0.2705
17	Western	14.34	51.51	3.59	242.51	871.12	507.35	0.2976
18	Himachal Pradesh	11.34	62.68	5.53	282.34	1560.59	746.93	0.4350
KARNATAKA		11.85	54.52	4.60	167.14	768.99	423.14	0.3154
19	Coastal and Ghat	14.89	50.03	3.36	283.86	953.76	571.91	0.2942
20	Inland Eastern	14.62	49.99	3.42	203.87	697.09	418.34	0.2744
21	Inland Southern	14.40	50.58	3.51	228.90	804.02	476.88	0.2903
22	Inland Northern	8.90	58.33	6.55	99.84	654.33	336.53	0.3156
KERALA		13.32	55.06	4.13	219.26	906.34	493.83	0.3376
23	Northern	13.81	54.03	3.91	212.11	829.85	460.77	0.3248
24	Southern	13.10	55.35	4.23	224.04	946.61	513.07	0.3426
MADHYA PRADESH		12.82	55.11	4.30	174.38	749.61	408.06	0.3266
25	Chattisgarh	13.97	52.78	3.78	191.06	721.84	410.29	0.3024
26	Vindhya	14.48	54.50	3.76	199.52	750.97	413.38	0.3191
27	Central	10.16	59.37	5.84	136.00	794.71	401.57	0.3629
28	Malwa	13.73	54.54	3.97	196.43	780.29	429.20	0.3309

(Contd.)

Table 4.2 *(Contd.)*

0	1	2	3	4	5	6	7	8
29	South	12.99	54.77	4.22	167.86	707.74	387.66	0.3226
30	South Western	7.52	60.06	7.99	90.74	724.72	362.00	0.3373
31	Northern	13.29	53.28	4.01	186.98	749.61	422.08	0.3123
MAHARASHTRA		11.16	56.69	5.08	197.09	1001.15	529.80	0.3510
32	Coastal	14.75	50.82	3.45	332.66	1146.14	676.59	0.2936
33	Inland Western	13.08	55.65	4.25	212.73	905.09	487.92	0.3358
34	Inland Northern	12.73	53.56	4.21	154.20	648.77	363.39	0.2948
35	Inland Central	5.07	65.67	12.95	65.23	844.84	385.95	0.4009
36	Inland Eastern	9.55	59.38	6.22	119.65	743.95	375.86	0.3504
37	Eastern	15.44	50.70	3.28	200.17	657.29	388.93	0.2641
ORISSA		12.30	53.83	4.38	165.04	722.29	402.54	0.3039
38	Coastal	12.38	55.02	4.44	155.90	692.87	377.79	0.3049
39	Southern	10.07	57.13	5.67	138.47	785.56	412.51	0.3460
40	Northern	13.98	51.07	3.65	199.38	728.36	427.86	0.2788
PUNJAB		15.64	49.56	3.17	266.26	843.73	510.73	0.2762
41	Northern	15.72	49.55	3.15	278.93	879.20	532.31	0.2729
42	Southern	15.49	49.63	3.20	243.39	779.84	471.39	0.2776
RAJASTHAN		14.26	51.60	3.62	201.89	730.54	424.73	0.2903
43	Western	16.67	48.71	2.92	241.66	706.15	434.91	0.2621
44	North Eastern	13.14	52.94	4.03	186.18	750.09	425.06	0.3014

(Contd.)

Table 4.2 *(Contd.)*

0	1	2	3	4	5	6	7	8
45	Southern	13.93	52.27	3.75	215.20	807.48	463.45	0.2970
46	South Eastern	12.84	53.61	4.18	163.81	683.96	382.74	0.3044
TAMIL NADU		12.57	55.83	4.44	183.64	815.66	438.29	0.3436
47	Coastal Northern	11.81	56.52	4.79	176.64	845.35	448.70	0.3492
48	Coastal	12.80	56.56	4.42	187.40	828.06	439.21	0.3556
49	Southern	12.80	54.64	4.27	160.44	684.89	376.04	0.3170
50	Inland	14.33	54.84	3.83	231.81	887.13	485.30	0.3387
UTTAR PRADESH		11.23	56.01	4.99	145.60	726.21	388.97	0.3229
51	Himalayan	15.07	48.52	3.22	256.30	825.18	510.21	0.2707
52	Western	10.95	56.64	5.17	154.21	797.68	422.50	0.3362
53	Central	11.76	55.02	4.68	143.89	673.21	367.07	0.3089
54	Eastern	12.94	52.55	4.06	152.64	619.86	353.87	0.2851
55	Southern	4.73	59.53	12.59	37.76	475.19	239.47	0.2417
WEST BENGAL		12.64	55.19	4.37	199.79	872.35	474.19	0.3342
56	Himalayan	14.05	50.43	3.59	157.07	563.77	335.38	0.2543
57	Eastern Plains	12.52	54.87	4.38	161.87	709.40	387.86	0.3166
58	Central Plains	12.96	54.34	4.19	220.93	926.35	511.42	0.3302
59	Western Plains	12.48	54.61	4.38	141.24	618.06	339.53	0.2974
	All India	13.55	54.66	4.03	206.86	834.48	458.05	0.3400

ratio in rural and urban areas are given in Table-4.1 and Table-4.2 respectively. Per capita consumption differ between the states, between the regions within a state, and also between sections of population. The ten regions with high and low per capita consumption in rural and urban areas are given below.

Regions with High and Low Consumption (Rs per capita per month)

Rural

Low Consumption		High Consumption	
1. Orissa Southern	(179.23)	1. Punjab Northern	(448.49)
2. M.P. South Western	(185.35)	2. Haryana Western	(437.30)
3. M.P. Central	(214.54)	3. Punjab Southern	(412.73)
4. Bihar Southern	(214.56)	4. Kerala Southern	(411.58)
5. Bihar Northern	(215.24)	5. Karnataka Coastal & Ghat	(368.91)
6. W.B. Himalayan	(217.11)	6. Maharashtra Coastal	(361.92)
7. U.P. Southern	(220.09)	7. Kerala Northern	(358.60)
8. Bihar Central	(225.77)	8. Himachal Pradesh	(350.63)
9. Orissa Coastal	(226.57)	9. Haryana Eastern	(349.22)
10. M.P. Chattisgarh	(227.29)	10.Rajasthan North-Eastern	(342.39)

Urban

Low Consumption		High Consumption	
1. U.P. Southern	(239.47)	1. Himachal Pradesh	(746.93)
2. Bihar Northern	(287.60)	2. Maharashtra Coastal	(676.59)
3. Bihar Central	(328.35)	3. Karnataka Coastal & Ghat	(571.91)
4. W.B. Himalayan	(335.38)	4. Gujarat Dry Areas	(563.33)
5. Karnataka Inland Northern	(336.58)	5. Punjab Northern	(532.31)
6. W.B. Western Plains	(339.53)	6. Kerala Southern	(513.07)
7. U.P. Eastern	(353.87)	7. Gujarat Southern Plains	(511.61)
8. A.P. Inland Southern	(359.71)	8. W.B. Central Plains	(511.42)
9. M.P. South West	(362.00)	9. U.P. Himalayan	(510.21)
10. Maharashtra Inland Northern	(363.39)	10. Haryana Western	(507.35)

N.B.: The figures in brackets are consumption expenditure, per capita per month.

In rural areas, eight of the ten low consumption regions are from the three less developed states, viz., Bihar, Orissa and Madhya Pradesh, whereas the ten urban regions with highest and lowest per capita consumption are scattered over seven and nine states respectively.

The per capita consumption of the regions within a state differs. In rural areas, the difference is substantial (around 50%) between (a) Southern and Northern Orissa, (b) Himalayan and Central Plains of West Bengal, (c) Coastal and Inland Northern Karnataka, (d) Western and Southern Uttar Pradesh, (e) South Eastern and Northern Madhya Pradesh, and (f) Coastal and Eastern Maharashtra. Such difference in urban areas are observed between: (a) Southern and Northern Bihar, (b) Dry Areas and Suarashtra region of Gujarat, (c) Himalayan and Central Plains of West Bengal, (d) Coastal and Inland Northern Karnataka, (e) Coastal and Inland Northern Maharashtra, and (f) Himalayan and Southern Uttar Pradesh.

Inequality

Just as per capita consumption differ between regions within a state, so does inequality. In rural areas, the Lorenz ratio in the regions within a state differs significantly between (a) South Western and Coastal Andhra Pradesh, (b) Southern Plains and Eastern Gujarat, (c) South and Chhatisgarh region and Central Madhya Pradesh, and (d) Southern and Western Rajasthan. In urban areas, such difference exists between (a) Hills and the remaining two regions in Assam, (b) Dry Areas and Saurashtra region in Gujarat, (c) Inland Central and Eastern Maharashtra, (d) Southern and Northern Orissa, (e) Western and Southern Uttar Pradesh, and (f) Central Plains and Himalayan West Bengal.

The inequality is high in the states witnessing high consumption. Also, most of the states and regions with low per capita consumption are classic examples of low inequality. Bihar, Orissa and to a great extent, Madhya Pradesh are cases of low growth and low inequality. The areas characterised by low per capita consumption and low inequality suffer from structural problems. The regions experiencing high growth and high inequality (HGHI) and low growth and low inequality (LGLI) in its extreme form are evident in rural areas. The urban regions, however, do not witness such a phenomenon.

The regions with HGHI in rural areas are Western Haryana, Inland Central Maharashtra and Southern and South-Eastern Rajasthan. Per capita consumption in these regions exceeds the national average by 17 to 55% and the Lorenz ratio by 10 to 34%. There are as many as 12 LGLI regions in rural areas. These are: Western Plains of Assam, Eastern Maharashtra, Himalayan West Bengal, all the three regions in Bihar and Orissa and three of the seven regions of Madhya Pradesh. Per capita consumption and Lorenz ratio in these regions are 10 to 35% less than the national average. However, Saurashtra region of Gujarat and North-Eastern Rajasthan turn out to be exceptions as these are the regions with high growth and low inequality.

The factors that determine the extent of inequality are not exactly known. Inequality has been generally observed to be low in regions with low per capita consumption in rural areas but not in urban areas. Ten regions with high and low inequality in rural and urban areas, measured by Lorenz ratio are given below.

Regions with High and Low Inequality
(Lorenz ratio)

Rural

Low Inequality		High Inequality	
1. W.B. Himalayan	(0.1497)	1. Maharashtra Inland Central	(0.3777)
2. Assam Hills	(0.1512)	2. M.P. South	(0.3640)
3. Assam Plain Western	(0.1753)	3. Tamil Nadu Coastal Northern	(0.3535)
4. Assam Plain Eastern	(0.1765)	4. A.P. South Western	(0.3370)
5. Orissa Southern	(0.2121)	5. Rajasthan Southern	(0.3289)
6. Gujarat Eastern	(0.2134)	6. Haryana Western	(0.3160)
7. M.P. Chattisgarh	(0.2149)	7. Rajasthan South-Eastern	(0.3100)
8. Bihar Northern	(0.2157)	8. U.P. Southern	(0.2983)
9. Gujarat Saurashtra	(0.2210)	9. Kerala Southern	(0.2885)
10. Bihar Central	(0.2236)	10. A.P. Inland Southern	(0.2870)

Urban

Low Inequality		High Inequality	
1. Assam Hills	(0.1918)	1. Himachal Pradesh	(0.4350)
2. Gujarat Saurashtra	(0.2177)	2. Maharashtra Inland Central	(0.4009)
3. U.P. Southern	(0.2417)	3. M.P. Central	(0.3629)
4. W.B. Himalayan	(0.2543)	4. Tamil Nadu Coastal	(0.3556)
5. Rajasthan Western	(0.2621)	5. Maharashtra Inland Eastern	(0.3504)
6. Maharashtra Eastern	(0.2641)	6. Gujarat Dry Areas	(0.3503)
7. Gujarat Eastern	(0.2675)	7. Tamil Nadu Coastal Northern	(0.3492)
8. Haryana Eastern	(0.2705)	8. Orissa Southern	(0.3460)
9. U.P. Himalayan	(0.2707)	9. Kerala Southern	(0.3426)
10. Bihar Central	(0.2729)	10. Tamil Nadu Inland	(0.3387)

N.B.: The figures in brackets are Lorenz Ratio of consumption distribution.

In rural areas, regions with low inequality are from the poorer states such as, Bihar, Orissa and Madhya Pradesh. Per capita consumption in nine of these ten regions are below the national average. On the other hand, only one of the ten rural regions with high inequality is from the poor states. And, per capita consumption of seven of these ten regions is about the national average. The ten urban regions with low inequality are scattered over as many as eight states.

The correlation coefficient between Lorenz ratio and fractile-wise consumption shares given below merely attests that reduction in inequality is possible by reducing the consumption share of top 30% of the population.

Correlation Between Consumption Shares

Correlation Between	Rural	Urban
1. Bottom and Top 30%	- 0.94	- 0.89
2. Bottom 30% and Lorenz Ratio	- 0.75	- 0.53
3. Top 30% and Lorenz Ratio	0.91	0.82

Inter-regional Variation in Consumption and Inequality

The regional spread of average consumption and its inequality in distribution is wide. At the national level, per capita consumption of bottom 30% of the population is less than half of that of all population and about one-fourth of that of top 30%. This is evident from the distribution of NSS regions by their deviation from the national average given below.

Consumption and Inequality: Deviation from National Average

I. Per Capita Consumption

Deviation from National Average (per cent)	All Rural	All Urban	Bottom 30% Rural	Bottom 30% Urban	Top 30% Rural	Top 30% Urban
1. -30% and less	2	2	3	7	2	5
2. - 20 to - 30%	5	8	5	5	10	10
3. - 10 to - 20%	12	16	9	10	10	18
4. 0 to - 10%	9	13	4	3	11	15
5. 0 to 10%	15	10	5	10	8	6
6. 10 to 20%	6	6	6	7	7	2
7. 20 to 30%	5	2	9	6	6	1
8. More than 30%	5	2	17	11	4	2
Total	59	59	58	59	58	59

II. Inequality

Deviation from National Average (%)	Number of Regions Rural	Number of Regions Urban
1. -20% and less	10	9
2. - 10 to - 20%	15	23
3. 0 to - 10%	19	18
4. 0 to + 10%	8	7
5. More than 10%	7	2
Total	59	59

The coefficient of variation of per capita consumption is not very different among the population groups or between rural and urban areas.

Variation in Consumption and Inequality

	Rural	Urban
I. Per Capita Consumption		
(a) Bottom 30%	27	29
(b) Top 30%	22	21
(c) All Population	20	19
II. Inequality (Lorenz Ratio)	17	13

The states in India are carved out following ethnicity and language as the principal criteria, with administrative convenience and efficiency as the pinnacle in the precipice. The diverse pattern of growth and inequality in some regions within the same state merely provide eyesight into the developmental process. These are nevertheless to act as important elements in the formulation of developmental policies, which ultimately affect the people, and their level of living.

Urban-Rural Disparity in Per Capita Consumption

The disparity in per capita consumption between rural and urban areas is indeed wide. The disparity is less for poor as compared to all population. Per capita total consumption in urban areas is 63% more than in rural in case of all population and 33% more in case of poor. The disparity is also less for food consumption, by 41% in case of all population and 26% in case of poor. These apart, there are urban-rural differential in the quality of food consumption. Such quality differential also exists between poor and non-poor within each area.

Distribution of Regions by Urban-Rural Disparity in Consumption

Urban-Rural Disparity	Bottom 30% Population	Top 30% Population	All Population
1. Negative	7	0	0
2. 0 to 20 %	16	6	7
3. 20 to 50 %	24	13	22
4. 50 to 100 %	10	31	28
5. 100 % +	1	8	2
Total	58	58	59

The urban-rural disparity in per capita consumption is greater in case of top 30% of the population as compared to bottom 30%. In eight regions, the per capita consumption of top 30% of the population in urban areas is twice of that in rural areas. However, in seven regions the per capita consumption of bottom 30% of the population in rural areas is more than in urban.

A low urban-rural disparity in per capita consumption can be due to both low rural and low urban consumption and high rural and high urban consumption. In 12 regions, the urban-rural disparity in per capita consumption is low (less than 50%) due to low per capita consumption in both the areas. Their deviation from the national averages are given below.

Low Urban-Rural Disparity due to Low Consumption in Both Areas

Region	Deviation in Rural (%)	Deviation in Urban (%)	Urban-Rural Disparity (%)
1. Bihar Northern	- 23.5	- 37.2	33.6
2. U.P. Southern	- 21.8	- 47.7	8.8
3. Bihar Central	- 19.8	- 28.3	45.4
4. Karnataka Inland Northern	- 12.2	- 26.5	36.2
5. U.P. Eastern	- 11.3	- 22.8	41.7
6. U.P. Central	- 10.6	- 19.9	46.0
7. Tamil Nadu Southern	- 8.4	- 17.9	45.8
8. Maharashtra Inland Central	- 6.8	- 15.8	47.2
9. M.P. South	- 3.6	- 15.4	43.0
10. W.B. Eastern Plains	- 3.2	- 15.3	42.4
11. A.P. Coastal	- 1.3	- 16.7	37.4
12. W.B. Western Plains	- 0.8	- 25.9	21.6

Per capita consumption in these 12 regions is up to 48% less than the national average in urban areas and 23% in rural areas. These regions are locked up in structural problems, and poverty and deprivation here are generally higher. In six regions, the urban-rural disparity in per capita consumption is low (31.8% and less) due to high per capita consumption in both the areas. Their deviations from the national averages are given below.

Low Urban-Rural Disparity due to High Consumption in Both Areas

Region	Deviation in Rural (%)	Deviation in Urban (%)	Urban-Rural Disparity (%)
1. Punjab Southern	46.7	2.9	14.2
2. Punjab Northern	59.4	16.2	18.7
3. Haryana Western	55.4	10.8	16.0
4. Kerala Southern	46.3	12.0	24.7
5. Haryana Eastern	24.1	0.5	31.8
6. Kerala Northern	27.4	0.6	28.5

The process of growth and development has been smooth and deprivation and poverty are less in these six regions where low urban-rural disparity is witnessed at the backdrop of high consumption in both the areas. In a way, these 18 regions outline the contrasts in the pattern of development. Special attention to development is needed in the regions where the disparity is high due to low consumption in both the areas. These regions are: Southern Bihar, Southern Orissa and South-Western, Chhattisgarh and Central Madhya Pradesh. Per capita consumption in these regions is 20 to 35% less than the national average in rural areas and 10 to 20% less in urban areas. These are low consumption regions and urban-rural disparity in these regions is high (more than 80%).

Food Share

About hundred years ago, Ernst Engel convincingly demonstrated that with increase in income, the proportion spent on food declines, if tastes and preferences remain unchanged. This inverse relationship between increase in household income/consumption and the fraction of it spent on food makes the latter an easily identifiable indicator for measuring the level of living. A derived analogy of this is the disproportionately high share of consumption utilised for food by the poor, and poor living is characterised by a large proportion of total consumption taken up by food. Foodgrain, within food consumption, is considered absolutely essential for sheer physical survival, and takes a disproportionately large share. The share of total expenditure spent on food at regional level given in Table-4.3 are able to convey a good deal of information about the level of living of the population.

The food share in rural areas is higher than in urban, and within each area, higher for poor as compared to non-poor. These shares in 1993-94 are about 20% point lower than they used to be twenty years ago (1973-74). Along with these declining shares, there has been a qualitative shift in the cereal consumption of the poor. For the poor group of population, the proportion of rice and wheat in cereal consumption (in quantity terms) is observed to increase from 64% in 1973-74 to 85% in 1993-94 in rural areas. The corresponding increase in urban areas is from 80% to 94%.

The coefficient of variation of food share among the regions is less than 10% and these are negatively associated with per capita consumption and the association is slightly stronger in the regions with below national average per capita consumption.

Distribution of Regions by Food Share (per cent of Total Consumption)

	Food Share (%)	Rural	Urban
1.	40 to 50	1	3
2.	50 to 60	14	45
3.	60 to 70	36	11
4.	70 +	8	0
	Total	59	59

The above analysis is based on cross-section data for the year 1993-94. A time series of food share constructed from the NSS consumer expenditure data of 12th to 53rd round, covering a 40 year period is given in Table-4.4. Table below gives the average food shares for different periods.

Temporal Food Shares

(Percentage)

	Period	Rural	Urban
1.	1956 to 1964	68 - 70	59 - 61
2.	1965 to 1973	73 - 77	64 - 67
3.	1977 to 1993	63 - 66	54 - 59
4.	1994 to 1997	59 - 61	50 - 53

Table 4.3 : Food Share in Regions

S.No. Regions		Rural	Urban
0	1	2	3
	ANDHRA PRADESH	59.57	53.83
1.	Coastal	61.53	55.00
2.	Inland Northern	58.17	51.85
3.	South Western	59.49	54.79
4.	Inland Southern	56.64	56.94
	ASSAM	72.25	59.68
5.	Plains Eastern	71.01	57.79
6.	Plains Western	72.91	60.98
7.	Hills	74.34	61.89
	BIHAR	71.00	62.90
8.	Southern	71.21	60.77
9.	Northern	70.14	65.73
10.	Central	72.05	64.42
	GUJARAT	67.10	58.41
11.	Eastern	66.98	62.87
12.	Plains Northern	66.50	56.78
13.	Plains Southern	64.42	56.77
14.	Dry Areas	66.92	48.55
15.	Saurashtra	69.55	65.98
	HARYANA	60.06	53.88
16.	Eastern	60.83	53.03
17.	Western	59.17	55.78
18.	Himachal Pradesh	60.02	42.48
	KARNATAKA	61.97	55.71
19.	Coastal and Ghat	59.51	57.85
20.	Inland Eastern	65.17	61.76
21.	Inland Southern	62.76	52.56
22.	Inland Northern	61.24	58.65
	KERALA	60.46	53.92
23.	Northern	60.60	54.35
24.	Southern	60.37	53.70
	MADHYA PRADESH	61.20	52.85
25.	Chattisgarh	66.71	55.64
26.	Vindhya	63.06	53.25

(Contd.)

Table 4.3 (*Contd.*)

0 1	2	3
27. Central	66.94	52.89
28. Malwa	60.54	50.39
29. South	50.70	52.33
30. South Western	61.94	52.28
31. Northern	57.73	54.09
MAHARASHTRA	59.48	53.02
32. Coastal	61.82	53.49
33. Inland Western	60.28	51.48
34. Inland Northern	65.59	58.18
35. Inland Central	50.80	47.13
36. Inland Eastern	59.58	53.79
37. Eastern	64.98	57.55
ORISSA	68.05	57.78
38. Coastal	66.83	56.22
39. Southern	71.09	57.38
40. Northern	68.43	59.54
PUNJAB	57.92	53.02
41. Northern	56.60	52.92
42. Southern	59.79	53.22
RAJASTHAN	62.29	56.66
43. Western	68.54	58.89
44. North Eastern	65.26	56.09
45. Southern	51.19	55.59
46. South Eastern	49.74	53.19
TAMIL NADU	62.83	54.61
47. Coastal Northern	59.58	54.96
48. Coastal	63.61	55.29
49. Southern	68.02	57.56
50. Inland	61.57	51.26
UTTAR PRADESH	61.45	55.99
51. Himalayan	63.90	53.72
52. Western	59.27	54.15
53. Central	60.24	56.81
54. Eastern	63.90	59.34
55. Southern	62.60	61.83

(*Contd.*)

Table 4.3 *(Contd.)*

0	1	2	3
	WEST BENGAL	66.83	55.92
56.	Himalayan	77.13	68.16
57.	Eastern Plains	65.83	59.64
58.	Central Plains	66.65	56.44
59.	Western Plains	65.22	63.90
	All India	63.17	54.65

Table 4.4 : Food Share at National Level

S.No.	NSS	Period	Rural	Urban
1.	12th	March, 1957 to Aug., 1957	70.3	58.4
2.	13th	Sept., 1957 to May 1958	68.3	59.9
3.	14th	July, 1958 to June, 1959	69.3	60.3
4.	15th	July, 1959 to June, 1960	68.1	61.0
5.	16th	July, 1960 to Aug., 1961	67.9	60.9
6.	17th	Sept., 1961 to July, 1962	68.8	60.2
7.	18th	Feb., 1963 to Jan., 1964	70.1	59.6
8.	20th	July, 1965 to June, 1966	74.0	63.8
9.	21st	July, 1966 to June, 1967	76.3	65.8
10.	22nd	July, 1967 to June, 1968	77.4	66.5
11.	23rd	July, 1968 to June, 1969	74.4	66.4
12.	24th	July, 1969 to June, 1970	73.8	65.7
13.	25th	July, 1970 to June, 1971	73.6	64.4
14.	27th	Oct., 1972 to Sept., 1973	72.7	64.4
15.	28th	Oct., 1973 to June, 1974	75.0	67.1
16.	32nd	July, 1977 to June, 1978	63.9	54.2
17.	38th	Jan., 1983 to Dec., 1983	65.6	59.1
18.	42nd	July, 1986 to June, 1987	65.6	57.9
19.	43rd	July, 1987 to June, 1988	63.3	56.0
20.	44th	July, 1988 to June, 1989	63.5	57.8
21.	45th	July, 1989 to June, 1990	64.3	55.5
22.	46th	July, 1990 to June, 1991	66.0	56.9
23.	47th	July, 1991 to Dec., 1991	63.1	56.1
24.	48th	Jan., 1992 to Dec., 1992	65.0	56.1
25.	49th	Jan., 1993 to June, 1993	65.2	57.7
26.	50th	July, 1993 to June, 1994	63.2	54.6
27.	51st	July, 1994 to June, 1995	61.0	53.2
28.	52nd	July, 1995 to June, 1996	60.4	50.1
29.	53rd	Jan., 1997 to Dec., 1997	58.7	49.6

Historically, the food share in rural areas is more than in urban areas by 9% point, which incidentally has been its decline in the past four decades (1956-1997). The increase in the food share from the first eight-year period (1956-1964) to second eight-year period (1965-1973) is due to the worsening of the economy during the three successive drought years.

The proportion of expenditure on food has often been used as a general measure of welfare. It has also been used by some as an alternative to the poverty ratio. This is a logical outcome of Engel's observation. By deciding a cut-off level of the proportion of total expenditure on food, persons or families spending more than this cut-off proportion have been treated as poor and those below as non-poor. It is a sufficiently vivid and easily quantifiable measure, besides being able to side-track the data and methodological complications associated with the estimation of poverty. However, it may be difficult to arrive at a consensus about the appropriate cut-off ratio of food expenditure. Engel's Law has been based on empirical observations made on relatively homogenous population, and it fails to take into account the influence of socio-cultural factors on food habits of the people, which is an important factor in determining the proportion of expenditure devoted to food. The criteria being sensitive to the choice of the cut-off value, any difference in the food habits, and hence in the food share, would affect its relationship with the poverty ratio severely. Therefore, in a multi-cultural heterogeneous country like India, the food share measure is unlikely to be a satisfactory substitute for the poverty ratio.

This observation is borne out by the data, which reveals that the association between food share and poverty indices in India is extremely weak. The ranking of the regions by food share and poverty indices (given in Chapter-5 and Chapter-6) differ enormously as can be seen from the rank correlation coefficients given below. It explodes the myth that food share can be able to replace the poverty indices or can be used as a proxy.

Rank Correlation Between Food Share and Poverty Indices

	Rank Correlation Between Food Share and:	Rural	Urban
1.	Very Poor	0.20	- 0.08
2.	Poverty Ratio	0.36	- 0.04
3.	Poverty Gap Ratio	0.26	- 0.03
4.	Squared Poverty Gap	0.20	- 0.11

It is appropriate, in the light of the recent findings that the analysis of food share should end with a caution. Recent studies have shown that Engel's observations may not always hold good for the poorest households in the developing economies. Yet, attempts have been made to use per capita food consumption to represent poverty and deprivation despite its weakness arising from the ignorance of non-food necessities such as, clothing, shelter and transport. Besides, it directly depends on the household's propensity to consume food, which may vary across the households.

5

POVERTY RATIO IN THE REGIONS

Keeping in view the importance of sub-state level poverty, these are estimated for 59 NSS regions falling within 16 major states, using the latest available NSS consumer expenditure data (50th Round) of the large survey, which is available for the year 1993-94. The state and region specific poverty ratios in rural and urban areas are estimated from the respective consumption distribution obtained from the NSS. The poverty line of the state is used for its regions. The poor are divided into: (a) very poor (VP), whose per capita consumption is less than three-fourth of the poverty line, and (b) moderately poor (MP), whose per capita consumption lie between three-fourth of the poverty line and the poverty line. The non-poor are classified into: (a) lower group (LNP), whose per capita consumption lie between poverty line and one and a half times of the poverty line and (b) upper group (UNP), whose per capita consumption exceeds one and a half times of the poverty line. The very poor may be living under cramping poverty, while the lower group of non-poor may belong to the straitened class. The region and state-specific percentage of people in the above categories in 1993-94 are given in Table-5.1 and Table-5.2 in rural and urban areas respectively.

Rural Poverty Ratio

Rural poverty ratio is high in Bihar and Orissa and low in Andhra Pradesh and Punjab. Among the ten regions with high (50 to 69%)

Table 5.1 : Poor and Non-Poor in Rural Regions

(*Percentage*)

Sl. No.	State/Regions	Very Poor	Moderately Poor	Poor	Lower Non-Poor	Upper Non-Poor	Non-Poor
0	1	2	3	4	5	6	7
	ANDHRA PRADESH	4.18	11.71	15.89	36.02	48.10	84.12
1	Coastal	4.50	12.76	17.26	37.13	45.61	82.74
2	Inland Northern	3.52	10.32	13.84	35.47	50.70	86.17
3	South Western	6.94	13.49	20.43	36.06	43.51	79.57
4	Inland Southern	2.51	10.36	12.87	32.53	54.59	87.12
	ASSAM	13.12	31.88	45.00	41.77	13.23	55.00
5	Plains Eastern	11.01	26.37	37.38	45.98	16.64	62.62
6	Plains Western	14.96	34.94	49.90	38.95	11.15	50.10
7	Hills	5.53	35.76	41.29	45.23	13.47	58.70
	BIHAR	27.67	30.50	58.17	29.62	12.21	41.83
8	Southern	31.57	30.87	62.44	24.83	12.74	37.57
9	Northern	27.62	31.06	58.68	30.21	11.12	41.33
10	Central	24.66	29.37	54.03	32.52	13.45	45.97
	GUJARAT	6.67	15.62	22.29	38.31	39.40	77.71
11	Eastern	10.42	15.47	25.89	35.60	38.51	74.11
12	Plains Northern	5.43	17.20	22.63	37.35	40.02	77.37
13	Plains Southern	8.80	19.90	28.70	38.52	32.78	71.30
14	Dry Areas	7.33	18.91	26.24	36.76	37.00	73.76
15	Saurashtra	2.90	8.90	11.80	42.91	45.28	88.19
	HARYANA	9.32	18.70	28.02	30.98	41.00	71.98
16	Eastern	10.03	21.88	31.91	32.65	35.44	68.09
17	Western	8.30	14.04	22.34	28.54	49.11	77.65
18	Himachal Pradesh	8.93	21.36	30.29	35.05	34.66	69.71
	KARNATAKA	11.11	18.78	29.89	36.06	34.05	70.11
19	Coastal and Ghat	2.86	6.38	9.24	30.90	59.86	90.76
20	Inland Eastern	4.47	9.23	13.70	43.44	42.87	86.31
21	Inland Southern	9.29	20.17	29.46	36.63	33.91	70.54

(*Contd.*)

Table 5.1 *(Contd.)*

0	1	2	3	4	5	6	7
22	Inland Northern	15.23	22.45	37.68	34.96	27.36	62.32
	KERALA	9.42	16.26	25.68	34.34	39.98	74.32
23	Northern	12.27	16.78	29.05	37.02	33.92	70.94
24	Southern	7.51	15.92	23.43	32.57	44.00	76.57
	MADHYA PRADESH	17.11	23.61	40.72	33.75	25.52	59.27
25	Chattisgarh	14.54	29.43	43.97	37.33	18.69	56.02
26	Vindhya	13.80	22.91	36.71	36.84	26.45	63.29
27	Central	21.78	28.35	50.13	35.38	14.49	49.87
28	Malwa	9.97	17.42	27.39	34.86	37.75	72.61
29	South	22.37	23.99	46.36	31.47	22.18	53.65
30	South Western	42.24	25.96	68.20	18.31	13.49	31.80
31	Northern	6.36	11.06	17.42	33.44	49.14	82.58
	MAHARASHTRA	16.17	21.73	37.90	32.41	29.69	62.10
32	Coastal	4.09	10.75	14.84	32.65	52.50	85.15
33	Inland Western	8.26	16.87	25.13	37.12	37.75	74.87
34	Inland Northern	19.11	28.07	47.18	33.38	19.44	52.82
35	Inland Central	28.91	21.11	50.02	25.54	24.44	49.98
36	Inland Eastern	20.06	29.02	49.08	31.76	19.15	50.91
37	Eastern	17.22	31.34	48.56	31.71	19.72	51.43
	ORISSA	21.77	28.02	49.79	33.21	17.00	50.21
38	Coastal	19.03	26.33	45.36	36.56	18.08	54.64
39	Southern	34.08	34.94	69.02	24.10	6.87	30.97
40	Northern	18.99	26.65	45.64	33.42	20.94	54.36
	PUNJAB	3.12	8.73	11.85	34.57	53.58	88.15
41	Northern	1.67	5.88	7.55	35.80	56.65	92.45
42	Southern	5.04	12.44	17.48	32.97	49.54	82.51
	RAJASTHAN	8.66	17.82	26.48	35.93	37.59	73.52
43	Western	5.84	19.64	25.48	40.23	34.28	74.51
44	North Eastern	5.78	12.01	17.79	35.93	46.29	82.22
45	Southern	16.05	29.87	45.92	33.44	20.64	54.08
46	South Eastern	16.18	18.56	34.74	28.50	36.76	65.26

(Contd.)

Table 5.1 *(Contd.)*

0	1	2	3	4	5	6	7
	TAMIL NADU	12.67	19.88	32.55	35.70	31.75	67.45
47	Coastal Northern	18.95	24.63	43.58	29.95	26.46	56.41
48	Coastal	6.15	13.67	19.82	37.31	42.88	80.19
49	Southern	15.48	21.26	36.74	37.39	25.88	63.27
50	Inland	6.01	16.65	22.66	40.40	36.94	77.34
	UTTAR PRADESH	19.55	22.76	42.31	32.20	25.48	57.68
51	Himalayan	7.05	17.93	24.98	43.59	31.43	75.02
52	Western	10.24	19.35	29.59	34.47	35.94	70.41
53	Central	26.79	23.41	50.20	29.13	20.67	49.80
54	Eastern	23.20	25.40	48.60	32.02	19.38	51.40
55	Southern	39.70	27.04	66.74	18.90	14.36	33.26
	WEST BENGAL	13.62	27.25	40.87	37.70	21.43	59.13
56	Himalayan	16.37	42.36	58.73	35.62	5.65	41.27
57	Eastern Plains	17.87	29.27	47.14	35.90	16.96	52.86
58	Central Plains	11.96	19.08	31.04	39.50	29.47	68.97
59	Western Plains	9.55	30.71	40.26	38.18	21.55	59.73
	All India	15.26	21.97	37.23	34.19	28.58	62.77

N.B.:

1. Very Poor = Percentage of persons below three-fourth of the poverty line.
2. Moderately Poor = Percentage of persons between three-fourth of the poverty line and the poverty line.
3. Poor = Percentage of persons below the poverty line.
4. Lower Non-Poor = Percentage of persons between the poverty line and one and a half times of the poverty line.
5. Upper Non-Poor = Percentage of persons above one and a half times of the poverty line.
6. Non-Poor = Percentage of persons above the poverty line.

Table 5.2 : Poor and Non-Poor in Urban Regions

(Percentage)

Sl. No.	State/Regions	Very Poor	Moderately Poor	Poor	Lower Non-Poor	Upper Non-Poor	Non-Poor
0	1	2	3	4	5	6	7
	ANDHRA PRADESH	16.78	21.56	38.34	28.19	33.47	61.66
1	Coastal	18.59	24.21	42.80	28.39	28.81	57.20
2	Inland Northern	12.22	18.25	30.47	29.00	40.53	69.53
3	South Western	20.29	20.64	40.93	24.74	34.32	59.06
4	Inland Southern	22.75	22.69	45.44	27.65	26.91	54.56
	ASSAM	1.16	6.58	7.74	29.06	63.20	92.26
5	Plains Eastern	0.00	4.42	4.42	24.27	71.31	95.58
6	Plains Western	1.88	8.23	10.11	32.61	57.28	89.89
7	Hills	1.57	2.29	3.86	21.75	74.38	96.13
	BIHAR	14.14	20.51	34.65	31.86	33.48	65.34
8	Southern	8.86	17.86	26.72	31.46	41.81	73.27
9	Northern	21.68	27.69	49.37	30.57	20.05	50.62
10	Central	15.49	19.09	34.58	33.13	32.29	65.42
	GUJARAT	11.18	16.75	27.93	34.95	37.13	72.08
11	Eastern	11.26	24.37	35.63	38.33	26.04	64.37
12	Plains Northern	12.22	15.37	27.59	31.89	40.51	72.40
13	Plains Southern	9.57	10.88	20.45	33.06	46.49	79.55
14	Dry Areas	9.79	17.39	27.18	24.60	48.22	72.82
15	Saurashtra	11.00	21.82	32.82	43.16	24.02	67.18
	HARYANA	5.02	11.35	16.37	29.29	54.33	83.62
16	Eastern	5.22	11.00	16.22	30.71	53.07	83.78
17	Western	4.53	12.22	16.75	25.75	57.49	83.24
18	Himachal Pradesh	1.13	8.09	9.22	25.11	65.66	90.77
	KARNATAKA	22.13	18.05	40.18	26.64	33.18	59.82
19	Coastal and Ghat	5.10	12.66	17.76	28.12	54.13	82.25
20	Inland Eastern	20.15	16.14	36.29	31.15	32.56	63.71
21	Inland Southern	12.56	16.52	29.08	28.41	42.51	70.92
22	Inland Northern	36.49	21.14	57.63	23.41	18.96	42.37
	KERALA	10.08	14.42	24.50	32.48	43.02	75.50
23	Northern	11.10	17.08	28.18	32.97	38.85	71.82

(Contd.)

Table 5.2 *(Contd.)*

0	1	2	3	4	5	6	7
24	Southern	9.51	12.87	22.38	32.19	45.43	77.62
	MADHYA PRADESH	25.69	22.66	48.35	28.03	23.61	51.64
25	Chattisgarh	21.88	22.32	44.20	31.44	24.35	55.79
26	Vindhya	24.32	26.13	50.45	25.65	23.91	49.56
27	Central	32.93	20.75	53.68	23.57	22.75	46.32
28	Malwa	21.85	23.68	45.53	30.03	24.43	54.46
29	South	27.90	23.33	51.23	28.51	20.26	48.77
30	South Western	36.60	20.54	57.14	19.26	23.60	42.86
31	Northern	23.54	21.18	44.72	28.72	26.55	55.27
	MAHARASHTRA	18.72	16.36	35.08	25.02	39.90	64.92
32	Coastal	4.04	9.07	13.11	26.68	60.21	86.89
33	Inland Western	17.02	23.41	40.43	27.46	32.11	59.57
34	Inland Northern	32.28	24.66	56.94	25.32	17.73	43.05
35	Inland Central	42.62	17.51	60.13	18.74	21.13	39.87
36	Inland Eastern	38.99	20.33	59.32	21.26	19.42	40.68
37	Eastern	21.02	31.00	52.02	23.57	24.41	47.98
	ORISSA	22.99	18.73	41.72	26.86	31.42	58.28
38	Coastal	26.54	21.88	48.42	25.79	25.79	51.58
39	Southern	33.53	12.11	45.64	17.84	36.52	54.36
40	Northern	15.00	17.46	32.46	31.38	36.16	67.54
	PUNJAB	2.22	9.18	11.40	27.71	60.88	88.59
41	Northern	1.67	6.82	8.49	26.72	64.79	91.51
42	Southern	3.25	13.49	16.74	29.51	53.74	83.25
	RAJASTHAN	12.98	17.55	30.53	32.18	37.30	69.48
43	Western	7.43	16.25	23.68	37.41	38.91	76.32
44	North Eastern	15.24	17.63	32.87	29.19	37.94	67.13
45	Southern	10.83	15.63	26.46	33.15	40.40	73.55
46	South Eastern	19.47	21.28	40.75	29.47	29.79	59.26
	TAMIL NADU	18.67	21.11	39.78	29.08	31.13	60.21
47	Coastal Northern	18.82	19.73	38.55	28.10	33.35	61.45
48	Coastal	20.31	21.80	42.11	28.08	29.81	57.89
49	Southern	24.82	23.31	48.13	28.45	23.43	51.88
50	Inland	11.06	21.02	32.08	32.07	35.86	67.93
	UTTAR PRADESH	16.91	18.43	35.34	29.62	35.05	64.67
51	Himalayan	5.49	12.00	17.49	21.34	61.17	82.51

(Contd.)

Table 5.2 *(Contd.)*

0	1	2	3	4	5	6	7
52	Western	14.37	16.66	31.03	29.47	39.50	68.97
53	Central	17.64	17.26	34.90	33.24	31.86	65.10
54	Eastern	18.48	20.12	38.60	31.53	29.87	61.40
55	Southern	37.54	34.98	72.52	16.59	10.88	27.47
	WEST BENGAL	7.51	14.87	22.38	27.81	49.82	77.63
56	Himalayan	13.27	19.50	32.77	38.27	28.97	67.24
57	Eastern Plains	12.12	20.65	32.77	29.18	38.05	67.23
58	Central Plains	5.30	12.76	18.06	26.60	55.34	81.94
59	Western Plains	17.84	22.51	40.35	31.62	28.03	59.65
	All India	14.85	17.42	32.28	28.83	38.89	67.72

N.B.: Notes are same as in Table 5.1

and low (7.5 to 17.5%) rural poverty, seven each are from three states. The high ones are from Bihar, Madhya Pradesh and Uttar Pradesh, and the low ones are from Andhra Pradesh, Punjab and Karnataka. Ten regions with high and low poverty in rural areas are given below.

Regions with High and Low Poverty Ratio:Rural

Low Poverty Ratio		High Poverty Ratio	
1. Punjab Northern	(7.55)	1. Orissa Southern	(69.02)
2. Karnataka Coastal & Ghat	(9.24)	2. M.P. South Western	(68.20)
3. Gujarat Saurashtra	(11.80)	3. U.P. Southern	(66.74)
4. A.P. Inland Southern	(12.87)	4. Bihar Southern	(62.44)
5. Karnataka Inland Eastern	(13.70)	5. W.B. Himalayan	(58.73)
6. A.P. Inland Northern	(13.84)	6. Bihar Northern	(58.68)
7. Maharashtra Coastal	(14.84)	7. Bihar Central	(54.03)
8. A.P. Coastal	(17.26)	8. U.P. Central	(50.20)
9. M.P. Northern	(17.42)	9. M.P. Central	(50.13)
10. Punjab Southern	(17.48)	10.Maharashtra Inland Central	(50.02)

N.B.: The figures in brackets are poverty ratio.

Rural poverty ratio in the regions within a state varies significantly in some cases. Examples are:

(a) In Gujarat, the incidence of poverty is 11.8% in Saurashtra region and 28.7% in Southern Plains.

(b) In Karnataka, 9.2% in Coastal and Ghat region and 37.7% in Northern Inland region.

(c) In Madhya Pradesh, 17.4% in Northern region and 68.2% in South West.

(d) In Maharashtra, 14.8% in Coastal region and 49.1% in Inland Eastern region.

(e) In Orissa, around 45% in Coastal and Northern region and 69% in Southern region.

(f) In Rajasthan, 17.8% in North-Eastern region and 45.9% in Southern region.

(g) In Tamil Nadu, 19.8% in Coastal region and 43.6% in Coastal Northern region.

(h) In Uttar Pradesh, 25% in Himalayan region and 66.7% in Southern region.

(i) In West Bengal, 31% in Central Plains and 58.7% in Himalayan region.

The regions with high poverty have a high percentage of very poor. The percentage of very poor in nine of the ten high poverty regions range from 22 to 42% as against the national rural average of 15.2%. The percentage of upper group of non-poor is low (about 15%) in regions with high poverty and high in regions with low poverty. Also, the percentage of upper group of non-poor in the regions differs significantly within some states. These are:

(a) In Karnataka, 27.4% in Inland Northern region and 59.9% in Coastal and Ghat region.

(b) In Madhya Pradesh, 13-14% in Central and South-West region and 49.1% in North.

(c) In Maharashtra, 17-20% in Inland Northern, Inland Eastern and Eastern region and 52.5% in Coastal region.

(d) In Rajasthan, 20.6% in South and 46.3% in North-East.

(e) In Uttar Pradesh, 14.4% in South and 35.9% in West.

(f) In West Bengal, 5.7% in Himalayan region and 29.5% in Central plains.

Urban Poverty Ratio

The urban poverty ratio of the 16 major states do not vary widely. But the variation among the 59 regions contained in these 16 states is wide. High urban poverty is concentrated in specific regions. It exceeds 50% in ten regions, of which eight are from two states, viz., Madhya Pradesh and Maharashtra. Ten regions with high and low poverty ratio in urban areas are given below.

Rgions with High and Low Poverty Ratio:Urban

Low Poverty Ratio		High Poverty Ratio	
1. Assam Hills	(3.86)	1. U.P. Southern	(72.52)
2. Assam Plain Eastern	(4.42)	2. Maharashtra Inland Central	(60.13)
3. Punjab Northern	(8.49)	3. Maharashtra Inland Eastern	(59.32)
4. Himachal Pradesh	(9.22)	4. Karnataka Inland Northern	(57.63)
5. Assam Plain Western	(10.11)	5. M.P. South Western	(57.14)
6. Maharashtra Coastal	(13.11)	6. Maharashtra Inland Northern	(56.94)
7. Haryana Eastern	(16.22)	7. M.P. Central	(53.68)
8. Punjab Southern	(16.74)	8. Maharashtra Eastern	(52.02)
9. Haryana Western	(16.75)	9. M.P. South	(51.23)
10. U.P. Himalayan	(17.49)	10. M.P. Vindhya	(50.45)

NB: The figures in brackets are poverty ratio.

Urban poverty ratio in the regions within a state varies significantly in some cases. Examples are:

(a) In Bihar, 26.7% in South and 49.4% in North.

(b) In Karnataka, 17.8% in Coastal and Ghat region and 57.6% in Inland Northern region.

(c) In Maharashtra, 13.1% in Coastal region and around 60% in Inland Central and Eastern region.

(d) In Uttar Pradesh, 17.5% in Himalayan region and 72.5% in South.

The regions within a state where the percentage of population in upper group of non-poor varies widely are:

(a) In Bihar, 20.1% in North and 41.8% in South.

(b) In Gujarat, 24% in Saurashtra region and 48.2% in Dry Areas.

(c) In Karnataka, 19% in Inland Northern region and 54.1% in Coastal and Ghat region.

(d) In Maharashtra, 17.7% in Inland Northern region and 60.2% in Coastal region.

(e) In Uttar Pradesh, 10.9% in South and 61.2% in Himalayan region.

(f) In West Bengal, 28% in Western Plains and 55.3% in Central Plains.

A Comparison of Rural and Urban Poverty

At the national level, rural poverty ratio is 5% points more than in urban. But the percentage of very poor is similar in the two areas. The rankings of rural and urban regions are also closer in case of percentage of very poor, the rank correlation coefficient being 0.52 as against 0.40 in case of poverty ratio. However, rural poverty ratio in 10 regions is less (at least two-third) than urban and five of these are from two southern states, viz., Andhra Pradesh and Karnataka, as can be seen from the Table below.

Rural and Urban Poverty Ratios

	State/Region	Rural	Urban
1.	Andhra Pradesh	15.89	38.34
	Coastal	17.26	42.80
	Inland Northern	13.84	30.47
	Inland Southern	12.87	45.44
2.	Gujarat	22.29	27.93
	Saurashtra	11.80	30.82
3.	Karnataka	29.89	40.18
	Inland Eastern	13.70	36.29
	Inland Northern	37.68	57.63
4.	Madhya Pradesh	40.72	48.35
	Malwa	27.39	45.53
	Northern	17.42	44.72
5.	Maharashtra	37.90	35.08
	Inland Western	25.13	40.43
6.	Tamil Nadu	32.55	39.78
	Coastal	19.82	42.11

The lower rural poverty in Andhra Pradesh is squarely due to low poverty line, which is the outcome of low prices, particularly of food. The price depressing effect of the Government sponsored food subsidy schemes is clearly at work in Andhra Pradesh, and also in Karnataka and Tamil Nadu.

Much of the urban poverty is presumed to be a spillover of rural poverty. The rise in the urban population by 3.2% per year as compared to 1.7% in rural since the mid-1970s is to a great extent due to persistent migration from the rural hinterland. Lower living standards in rural areas force rural to urban migration, leading to overcrowding in unskilled and low paid jobs in urban informal sector and in turn, rapid growth of pockets of poverty in many cities and towns.

Consumption, Inequality and Poverty

The correlates of poverty are not the same in all regions. This is evident from the characteristics of the regions with high and low poverty, and the poverty situation in regions with high and low consumption and inequality.

Regions with High and Low Poverty

Per capita consumption in both high (50 to 69%) and low (7.5 to 17.5%) poverty regions is wide, differing by 46% and 61% respectively between the maximum and the minimum. Per capita consumption in the ten high poverty regions range from 64 to 80% of the national average. The inequality in the ten low poverty regions is spread over a rather narrow range, whereas it is wide in the high poverty regions. The region with highest poverty is also the region with lowest consumption.

Consumption and Inequality in Regions with High and Low Poverty

	Ten Regions with Low Poverty Ratio	Ten Regions with High Poverty Ratio
I. Rural		
1. Number of States	6	6
2. Per Capita Consumption	Rs. 278 to Rs 448	Rs 179 to Rs 262
3. Lorenz Ratio	0.22 to 0.29	0.15 to 0.38
4. Very Poor (%)	1.67 to 6.36	16.37 to 42.24
5. Poverty Ratio (%)	7.5 to 17.5	50 to 69
II. Urban		
1. No of States	5	4
2. Per Capita Consumption	Rs. 431 to Rs 677	Rs 239 to Rs 413
3. Lorenz Ratio	0.19 to 0.29	0.24 to 0.40
4. Very Poor (%)	0 to 5.49	21.02 to 42.62
5. Poverty ratio (%)	3.9 to 17.7	50 to 72.5

Rural poverty ratio exceeds 45% in twenty regions and sixteen of these are from five states, with four from Maharashtra and three each from Bihar, Orissa, Madhya Pradesh and Uttar Pradesh. Per capita consumption in 19 of these 20 regions is less than the national rural average, and in 15 the inequality is low.

Two issues surface from the nature and pattern of rural poverty described above. First, high rural poverty is concentrated in specific regions. Secondly, a wide range of per capita consumption characterises the poverty scenario and it is the lack of purchasing power rather than its inequitable distribution that causes high poverty.

In ten regions with high urban poverty, the poverty ratios range from 50 to 72.5%. Of these, eight come evenly from Madhya Pradesh and Maharashtra. Per capita consumption and its inequality in distribution vary widely in these ten regions. Per capita consumption and inequality are also widely spread in the ten regions with low urban poverty.

High and Low Consumption Regions

The poverty ratios of ten regions with high and low per capita consumption are summarised below.

Poverty and Inequality in High and Low Consumption Regions

	Ten Regions with Low Per Capita Consumption	Ten Regions with High Per Capita Consumption
I. Rural		
1. Number of States	5	7
2. Per Capita Consumption	Rs. 179 to Rs 227	Rs 336 to Rs 482
3. Lorenz Ratio	0.1497 to 0.2983	0.2324 to 0.3160
4. Very Poor (%)	14.54 to 42.24	1.67 to 12.27
5. Poverty Ratio (%)	43.97 to 69.02	7.55 to 31.91
II. Urban		
1. No of States	7	9
2. Per Capita Consumption	Rs. 239 to Rs 363	Rs 503 to Rs 677
3. Lorenz Ratio	0.2417 to 0.3373	0.2707 to 0.3503
4. Very Poor (%)	13.27 to 37.54	0 to 9.79
5. Poverty ratio (%)	32.77 to 72.52	4.42 to 27.18

Per capita consumption in low consumption regions ranges from 50 to 80% of the national average. The range of poverty ratio and the percentage of very poor is wide in these regions. The difference in the percentage of poor and very poor in some of these regions point towards the fact that the growth in per capita consumption beyond a certain threshold rate is a necessary pre-condition to have profound impact on reduction of poverty and immiserisation.

Regions with High and Low Inequality

The poverty ratio in ten regions with high and low inequality is summarised below.

Poverty ratios vary widely in regions with both high and low inequality. In fact, regions with low inequality contain some of the high poverty regions. This is true in both rural and urban areas. The range of per capita consumption in low inequality regions is similar in rural and urban areas whereas in high inequality regions it is wide in rural areas as compared to urban. Generally, regions with low inequality have low per capita consumption and high poverty. The regions with high inequality though have high per capita consumption, are a mix of high and low poverty.

Consumption and Poverty in Regions with High and Low Inequality

	Ten Regions with Low Inequality	Ten Regions with High Inequality
I. Rural		
1. Number of States	6	8
2.Per Capita Consumption	Rs. 179 to Rs 327	Rs 220 to Rs 437
3. Lorenz Ratio	0.1497 to 0.2236	0.2870 to 0.3777
4. Poverty Ratio (%)	11.81 to 69.02	12.89 to 66.74
II. Urban		
1. No of States	8	6
2.Per Capita Consumption	Rs. 239 to Rs 510	Rs 362 to Rs 563
3. Lorenz Ratio	0.1918 to 0.2729	0.3373 to 0.4009
4. Poverty ratio (%)	3.86 to 72.52	22.38 to 60.13

Regional Variation in Poverty

The poverty ratios in 59 regions range from a low of 7.5 to a high of 69% in rural areas and from 3.9 to 72.5% in urban areas. The national average of the percentage of population in different groups along with their indicators of regional dispersion are given below.

Population by Categories:Average and Variation

	Very Poor	Moderately Poor	Poor	Lower Non-Poor	Upper Non-Poor	Non-Poor
I. Rural						
(a) Average	15.2	22.0	37.2	34.2	28.6	62.8
(b) Minimum	1.7	5.9	7.5	18.3	5.7	31.0
(c) Maximum	42.2	42.4	69.0	46.0	59.9	92.4
(d) C.V.	68	38	45	14	45	23
II. Urban						
(a) Average	14.9	17.4	32.3	28.8	38.9	67.7
(b) Minimum	0.0	2.3	3.9	17.8	10.9	27.5
(c) Maximum	42.6	35.0	72.5	43.2	71.3	96.1
(d) C.V.	63	34	44	17	39	23

The regional variation of the percentage of population in each group is almost identical in rural and urban areas. The percentage of very poor is widely dispersed. The distribution of regions by poverty ratio and percentage of very poor given below is a summary assessment of the regional variation in the incidence of poverty.

Distribution of Regions by Poverty

Poverty Ratio/ Very Poor (%)	Poverty Ratio Rural	Very Poor Rural	Poverty Ratio Urban	Very Poor Urban
0 to 10	2	27	4	17
10 to 20	10	20	8	21
20 to 30	15	8	9	13
30 to 40	8	3	14	7
40 to 50	14	1	14	1
50 +	10	0	10	0
Total	59	59	59	59

In four-fifth of the regions the percentage of very poor is less than 20% in rural areas and 30% in urban areas. The poverty ratio is concentrated in 10 to 30% range in rural areas and 30 to 50% in urban. The correlation coefficients between the percentage of population in different groups given below is a quantification of their association at regional level.

Correlation Matrix of Poverty

I.Rural	VP	MP	Poor	LNP	UNP	Non-Poor
1.Very Poor	1.00	0.68	0.92	- 0.67	- 0.78	- 0.92
2.Moderately Poor		1.00	0.91	- 0.16	- 0.96	- 0.91
3. Poor			1.00	- 0.46	- 0.95	- 1.00
4. Lower Non-Poor				1.00	0.15	0.46
5.Upper Non-Poor					1.00	0.95
6.Non-Poor						1.00
II.Urban						
1.Very Poor	1.00	0.67	0.95	- 0.41	- 0.85	- 0.95
2.Moderately Poor		1.00	0.86	0.02	- 0.90	- 0.86
3. Poor			1.00	- 0.27	- 0.94	- 1.00
4. Lower Non-Poor				1.00	- 0.06	0.27
5.Upper Non-Poor					1.00	0.95
6.Non-Poor						1.00

The correlation coefficient of poor and non-poor with other categories of population connote the following.

(a) The regions with high percentage of poor have high percentage of very poor and *vice-versa*.

(b) The regions with high percentage of non-poor have high percentage of upper group of non-poor.

(c) The regions with low poverty ratio or low percentage of very poor have a greater percentage of population in upper group of non-poor.

Concentration of Population and Poor

India's distribution of population among its 32 States and Union Territories (UT) is such that:

(a) 98% of the population is concentrated in eighteen states/UTs.

(b) More than 80% of the population live in ten states.

The area of each state/UT has distinct components of rural and urban. The concentration of population bears hardly any urban-rural discrepancy. However, in a few areas the concentration is slightly different as:

(a) Uttar Pradesh and Bihar account for 30% of the rural population, and

(b) Uttar Pradesh and Maharashtra account for 25% of the urban population.

The poor across the states are equally concentrated. The concentration of rural poor is such that:

(a) 38.8% live in Uttar Pradesh and Bihar.

(b) 25.4% live in Madhya Pradesh, Maharashtra and West Bengal.

(c) 96.2% live in 14 states.

The concentration of urban poor is such that:

(a) 50% of them live in four states, viz., Madhya Pradesh, Maharashtra, Tamil Nadu and Uttar Pradesh.

(b) 90% live in ten states.

For the state as a whole (rural and urban combined), it is observed that:

(a) More than one-third (34%) of the poor live in Bihar and Uttar Pradesh,

(b) Another one-fourth (27%) live in Madhya Pradesh, Maharashtra and West Bengal.

(c) Fifteen states account for 95.5% of the poor.

The concentration of poor may be viewed from an alternative angle. Poverty ratio exceeds 60% in four rural regions and in two urban regions spread over five states, viz., Bihar, Madhya Pradesh, Orissa, Maharashtra and Uttar Pradesh. India's 5.23% of rural population and 2% of urban population (or 4.4% of India's total population) live in these regions. Since the average poverty ratio of these six regions is 65%, 25.3 million people (22.3 million in rural and 3 million in urban) live in areas affected by abject poverty.

6

THE DEPTH AND SEVERITY OF POVERTY

It has already been mentioned in Chapter-2 that the poverty ratio is inadequate in picturising the depth and severity of poverty since it does not distinguish between people below the poverty line nor the effort required to raise them out of poverty. Although an indication has been provided at the national level in Chapter-2, regional variations are also of considerable significance. In view of this, the distributional indices of poverty, such as the Poverty Gap Ratio (PGR) and the Squared Poverty Gap (SPG) have been computed here in order to have an idea about the depth and severity of poverty. These are computed at the state and NSS region level in rural and urban areas from the respective consumption distribution of the NSS. The state-wise poverty lines are used for the regions within the state for estimation of regional poverty indices. Two things are done here. First, from a comparison of poverty ratio, PGR and SPG, the inadequacy of poverty ratio in capturing depth and severity of poverty in the states/regions is highlighted. Second, comparing the Contribution to Total Poverty (CTP) computed from the SPG, and Share of Poor (SP) from the poverty ratio, it is advocated that CTP be used for allocation of funds under anti poverty programmes instead of share of poor. The Poverty Ratio, Poverty Gap Ratio and Squared Poverty Gap at region and state-level are given in Table-6.1.

At the national level, the poverty ratio is more in rural areas (37.2%) as compared to urban (32.3%). In both rural and urban

Table 6.1 : Poverty Indices in the Regions

States	Region	Rural Poverty Ratio	Rural Poverty Gap Ratio	Rural Squared Poverty Gap	Urban Poverty Ratio	Urban Poverty Gap Ratio	Urban Squared Poverty Gap
1	2	3	4	5	6	7	8
Andhra Pradesh	Coastal	17.26	3.1827	0.9098	42.80	10.2292	3.5619
	Inland Northern	13.84	2.2100	0.5720	30.47	6.5380	2.0558
	South Western	20.43	4.2944	1.3543	40.93	10.9324	4.1625
	Inland Southern	12.87	2.1230	0.4959	45.44	11.6508	4.1307
	Total	15.89	2.8284	0.7861	38.34	9.0689	3.1170
Assam	Plain Eastern	37.38	6.7807	1.8326	4.42	0.1078	0.0252
	Plain Western	49.90	9.2265	2.4576	10.11	1.1780	0.3301
	Hills	41.29	5.5081	1.0173	3.86	0.7045	0.1863
	Total	45.00	8.1810	2.1687	7.74	0.7537	0.2086
Bihar	Southern	62.44	16.1220	5.5061	26.72	5.0554	1.4897
	Northern	58.68	14.7790	5.0692	49.37	11.7550	4.0373
	Central	54.03	13.1671	4.4113	34.58	8.1574	2.7565
	Total	58.17	14.6123	4.9739	34.65	7.6841	2.5193
Gujarat	Eastern	25.89	5.3437	1.5371	35.63	6.3885	1.7650
	Plain Northern	22.63	3.7575	0.9539	27.59	6.2680	1.9857

(Contd.)

Table 6.1 *(Contd.)*

1	2	3	4	5	6	7	8
	Plain Southern	28.70	5.1947	1.5581	20.45	4.9595	1.7804
	Dry Areas	26.24	4.3375	1.1693	27.18	6.2514	2.0001
	Saurashtra	11.80	2.0006	0.6809	32.82	6.4655	1.9270
	Total	22.29	3.9832	1.1204	27.93	6.0692	1.9178
Haryana	Eastern	31.91	6.3278	1.9837	16.22	3.0364	0.8804
	Western	22.34	4.4834	1.3018	16.75	2.7051	0.6764
	Total	28.02	5.5760	1.7054	16.37	3.0137	0.8208
Himachal	Pradesh	30.29	5.5279	1.5900	9.22	1.1534	0.2400
Karnataka	Coastal & Ghat	9.24	1.2631	0.2889	17.76	2.8347	0.9004
	Inland Eastern	13.70	2.5619	0.8532	36.29	9.2140	3.0810
	Inland Southern	29.46	5.6907	1.7176	29.08	6.5401	2.0506
	Inland Northern	37.68	8.1970	2.6236	57.63	18.5569	7.6765
	Total	29.89	6.1753	1.9372	40.18	11.2584	4.2805
Kerala	Northern	29.05	6.6838	2.3816	28.18	5.8474	1.9522
	Southern	23.43	4.7165	1.4567	22.38	4.9751	1.7905
	Total	25.68	5.5032	1.8269	24.50	5.2896	1.8467
Madhya	Chattisgarh	43.97	8.4994	2.4041	44.20	11.3885	4.0406
Pradesh	Vindhya	36.71	7.6394	2.2888	50.45	12.1359	3.8878
	Central	50.13	11.8357	3.8813	53.68	17.0649	7.1517
	Malwa	27.39	5.4698	1.6382	45.53	11.3121	3.8311

(Contd.)

Table 6.1 *(Contd.)*

1	2	3	4	5	6	7	8
	South	46.36	11.7291	4.0898	51.23	14.5618	5.5420
	South Western	68.20	22.5878	9.6780	57.14	19.6619	8.8297
	Northern	17.42	3.5049	1.1057	44.72	11.8866	4.3248
	Total	40.72	9.4145	3.1557	48.35	13.3183	4.9870
Maharashtra	Coastal	14.84	2.4293	0.6286	13.11	2.2825	0.6699
	Inland Western	25.13	4.9305	1.5308	40.43	9.7072	3.5379
	Inland Northern	47.18	10.8231	3.5295	56.94	16.6750	6.6407
	Inland Central	50.02	15.8563	6.6877	60.13	22.8915	11.0036
	Inland Eastern	49.08	11.3889	3.5752	59.32	19.8663	8.6218
	Eastern	48.56	10.5812	3.2496	52.02	12.1935	4.2684
	Total	37.90	9.2059	3.2283	35.08	10.0118	4.1018
Orissa	Coastal	45.36	10.2119	3.2217	48.42	12.9281	4.5157
	Southern	69.02	18.7872	6.8299	45.64	14.9915	6.2900
	Northern	45.64	10.4150	3.4392	32.46	7.9624	3.1394
	Total	49.79	11.8310	3.9534	41.72	11.2602	4.2157
Punjab	Northern	7.55	1.0646	0.2557	8.49	1.0714	0.2720
	Southern	17.48	2.9611	0.7533	16.74	2.5460	0.6044
	Total	11.85	1.8838	0.4682	11.40	1.5892	0.3884
Rajasthan	Western	25.49	4.1523	1.1723	23.68	4.0114	1.1250
	North-Eastern	.17.79	3.3819	1.0341	32.87	7.8132	2.5749

(Contd.)

Table 6.1 *(Contd.)*

1	2	3	4	5	6	7	8
	Southern	45.92	9.6524	2.8565	26.46	5.7207	1.9467
	South-Eastern	34.74	7.8257	2.5374	40.75	10.3806	3.6391
	Total	26.48	5.1027	1.5355	30.53	6.7838	2.1998
Tamil Nadu	Coastal Northern	43.58	10.3744	3.5538	38.55	10.3391	4.2175
	Coastal	19.82	3.9442	1.2802	42.11	10.5064	3.6594
	Southern	36.74	8.6242	2.9579	48.13	12.9876	4.8995
	Inland	22.66	3.8250	1.0993	32.08	6.0535	1.7919
	Total	32.55	7.2066	2.4047	39.78	10.0246	3.7689
Uttar Pradesh	Himalayan	24.98	4.2891	1.0646	17.49	3.1727	0.8714
	Western	29.59	6.0245	1.8142	31.03	7.6489	2.7090
	Central	50.20	13.7247	4.9439	34.90	9.4195	3.4820
	Eastern	48.60	11.9119	3.9663	38.60	9.2524	3.0913
	Southern	66.74	20.1221	7.9559	72.52	20.8858	7.9317
	Total	42.31	10.3092	3.4777	35.34	8.9314	3.1628
West Bengal	Himalayan	58.73	11.3466	3.1322	32.77	7.2815	2.3786
	Eastern Plains	47.14	9.9821	3.0958	32.77	6.9145	2.1512
	Central-Plains	31.04	6.6084	2.0605	18.06	3.2526	1.0064
	Western-Plains	40.26	6.7556	1.7739	40.35	9.1514	2.6708
	Total	40.87	8.1372	2.4115	22.38	4.3666	1.3430

areas, the poverty ratio is less dispersed among the regions than poverty gap ratio, which again is less dispersed than the squared poverty gap.

Average and Variability of Regional Poverty Indices

	Rural	Urban
I Average		
1. Poverty Ratio	37.23	32.28
2. Poverty Gap Ratio	8.43	7.84
3. Squared Poverty Gap	2.77	2.81
II. Inter-Regional Variation (%)		
1. Poverty Ratio	45	44
2. Poverty Gap Ratio	62	61
3. Squared Poverty Gap	76	74

Poverty Gap Ratio

The depth of poverty measured by Poverty Gap Ratio is more widely spread between the regions within a state as compared to the poverty ratio. In the regions mentioned below, the poverty ratios are not able to capture the depth of poverty adequately.

I. *Poverty Ratio overstates the Depth of Poverty*

(a) Rural Areas : Inland Northern, Inland Eastern and Eastern Maharashtra, Southern Punjab, Southern Rajasthan, Western Plains and Himalayan region of West Bengal and Eastern Uttar Pradesh.

(b) Urban Areas: Eastern and Saurashtra region of Gujarat, Western Haryana, Coastal and Ghat region of Karnataka, Southern Punjab, Himalayan Uttar Pradesh and Central Plains of West Bengal.

II. *Poverty Ratio fails to capture the Depth of Poverty*

(a) *Rural Areas :* South Western Madhya Pradesh, Inland Central Maharashtra, Southern Orissa, Central and Southern Uttar Pradesh.

(b) *Urban Areas :* Inland Northern Karnataka, Central and South-Western Madhya Pradesh, Southern Orissa and Inland Central and Inland Eastern Maharashtra.

Squared Poverty Gap

The regional disparity in Squared Poverty Gap is wider than poverty ratio or poverty gap ratio, and hence the spread of the severity of poverty. A comparison of poverty ratio and SPG given below reveals the failure of poverty ratio to adequately capture the phenomenon of severity of poverty. The rural regions, where the poverty ratios are similar (around 50%) but the SPG differ by at least three times, are : Inland Central and Inland Eastern Maharashtra, Central Uttar Pradesh, Central Madhya Pradesh and Western Plains of Assam. There are also regions where similar poverty ratios are accompanied by wide difference in the SPG. These are: (a) Inland Southern Andhra Pradesh and Saurashtra region of Gujarat, (b) Northern Kerala and Inland Southern Karnataka, (c) Eastern Plains of Assam and Southern Tamil Nadu.

In urban areas, similar poverty ratios with widely different SPG are observed in:

(a) Saurashtra region of Gujarat and Northern Orissa
(b) Eastern Gujarat and Inland Eastern Karnataka
(c) South Western Andhra Pradesh and Western Plains of West Bengal
(d) Inland Southern Andhra Pradesh and Southern Orissa
(e) South Western Madhya Pradesh and Inland Northern Maharashtra

Contribution to Total Poverty

SPG is additively decomposable with share of population in the sub-groups as weights. This, while allowing disaggregation of total poverty into poverty of sub-groups, can provide a quantitative assessment of the effect of a change in the sub-group poverty to total poverty or the sub-group contribution to total poverty by viewing the total poverty as a weighted average of sub-group poverty. The sub-groups can be carved out as regions or occupation and socio-economic groups.

The property of additive decomposability of SPG is used to measure the contribution of each state in the national poverty and also of each region in the state poverty. The measure of Contribution to Total Poverty (CTP) is compared with the region and state-specific Share of Poor (SP), computed from the poverty ratio. A comparison of CTP and SP can help in tracing the areas or groups of population afflicted with severity of poverty.

The allocation of funds under anti-poverty programmes based on poverty ratio, *inter-alia*, the share of poor is at the disadvantage of the states/regions where CTP is more than SP, i.e., in (I) above while unduly benefiting the states in (II) where CTP is less than SP. A well planned attack on poverty requires more attention to the regions where CTPs exceed share of poor. The allocation of funds under anti-poverty programmes based on CTP rather than share of poor can help in reaching these areas in a more subtle fashion. By not considering severity of poverty, certain regions are unduly benefitted in the matter of allocation of funds under anti-poverty programmes.

The areas with high SPG, implying greater severity of poverty should be the target of anti-poverty programmes, aiming to generate income for the poor directly, bypassing the general growth process. The allocation of funds under anti-poverty programmes among the states should ideally be made on the basis of CTP instead of the share of poor. The earmarking of funds at sub-state level can be based on the regional CTPs. If need be, special schemes can also be formulated for sub-groups of the population. This analytical refinement in measuring the incidence of poverty through SPG and its use in the allocation of funds under anti-poverty programmes is appropriate in devising the operational strategy for tackling the problem of poverty.

CTP and SP at State Level

The CTP and SP in rural and urban areas at state level are given in Table-6.2.

Table 6.2 : CTP and SP in the States

(Percentage)

		Rural		Urban	
S.No.	State	CTP	SP	CTP	SP
0	1	2	3	4	5
1.	Andhra Pradesh	2.16	3.29	9.15	9.79
2.	Assam	2.51	3.91	0.08	0.27
3.	Bihar	21.24	18.67	4.69	5.61
4.	Gujarat	1.73	2.59	4.61	5.66
5.	Haryana	1.23	1.51	0.55	0.96
6.	Himachal Pradesh	0.44	0.64	0.02	0.06
7.	Karnataka	3.43	3.98	9.74	7.96
8.	Kerala	2.19	2.31	2.33	2.68
9.	Madhya Pradesh	9.26	8.97	12.82	10.82
10.	Maharashtra	9.07	8.00	19.73	14.68
11.	Orissa	6.18	5.85	3.01	2.59
12.	Punjab	0.38	0.73	0.38	0.97
13.	Rajasthan	3.03	3.93	3.69	4.45
14.	Tamil Nadu	4.97	5.05	11.51	10.57
15.	Uttar Pradesh	22.50	20.58	14.62	14.21
16.	West Bengal	6.84	8.71	4.04	5.86

Given below are the wide differences between CTP and SP at state level.

I. CTP greater than SP:

(a) Rural and Urban : Maharashtra, Madhya Pradesh;
(b) Rural : Bihar, Uttar Pradesh, Orissa;
(c) Urban: Karnataka

II. CTP less than SP:

(a) Rural and Urban: Andhra Pradesh, Assam, Gujarat, Punjab, West Bengal;
(b) Urban: Bihar, Rajasthan

Table 6.3 : CTP and SP in the Regions

(Percentage)

		Rural		Urban	
States	Region	CTP	SP	CTP	SP
0	1	2	3	4	5
Andhra Pradesh	Coastal	50.83	47.88	46.75	48.70
	Inland Northern	27.17	32.61	35.88	30.29
	South Western	16.39	12.27	9.28	11.81
	Inland Southern	5.61	7.24	8.09	9.20
	Total	100.00	100.00	100.00	100.00
Assam	Plain Eastern	41.23	39.91	21.09	4.38
	Plain Western	55.16	53.14	75.75	90.06
	Hills	3.61	6.95	3.16	5.56
	Total	100.00	100.00	100.00	100.00
Bihar	Southern	25.42	24.64	31.38	24.01
	Northern	47.19	46.69	33.02	37.05
	Central	27.39	28.67	35.60	38.94
	Total	100.00	100.00	100.00	100.00
Gujarat	Eastern	27.91	24.03	22.07	16.93
	Plain Northern	20.11	24.41	33.37	37.16
	Plain Southern	21.49	20.23	8.39	11.30
	Dry Areas	16.48	18.91	7.53	8.58
	Saurashtra	14.01	12.42	28.64	26.03
	Total	100.00	100.00	100.00	100.00
Haryana	Eastern	69.07	67.66	71.65	77.27
	Western	30.93	32.34	28.35	22.73
	Total	100.00	100.00	100.00	100.00
Karnataka	Coastal and Ghat	1.39	2.88	3.41	1.65
	Inland Eastern	5.68	5.90	6.79	5.48
	Inland Southern	26.77	29.73	34.81	23.32
	Inland Northern	66.16	61.49	54.99	69.55
	Total	100.00	100.00	100.00	100.00
Kerala	Northern	54.65	47.76	44.75	41.22
	Southern	45.35	52.24	55.25	58.78
	Total	100.00	100.00	100.00	100.00

(Contd.)

Table 6.3 *(Contd.)*

0	1	2	3	4	5
Madhya	Chattisgarh	21.86	30.95	18.10	15.48
Pradesh	Vindhya	10.69	13.27	9.81	7.07
	Central	10.62	10.62	15.85	19.75
	Malwa	8.11	10.50	20.60	16.21
	South	17.01	14.93	8.66	8.77
	South Western	28.09	15.32	15.34	22.18
	Northern	3.62	4.41	11.64	10.54
	Total	100.00	100.00	100.00	100.00
Maharashtra	Coastal	2.20	4.44	17.29	7.68
	Inland Western	13.49	18.92	22.61	17.20
	Inland Northern	15.23	17.39	14.98	15.18
	Inland Central	42.36	27.08	16.04	25.50
	Inland Eastern	18.85	22.11	24.91	31.47
	Eastern	7.87	10.06	4.17	2.97
	Total	100.00	100.00	100.00	100.00
Orissa	Coastal	38.50	43.07	57.71	53.87
	Southern	31.40	25.21	12.65	17.44
	Northern	30.10	31.72	29.64	28.69
	Total	100.00	100.00	100.00	100.00
Punjab	Northern	29.82	35.09	47.35	44.40
	Southern	70.18	64.91	52.65	55.60
	Total	100.00	100.00	100.00	100.00
Rajasthan	Western	26.53	33.09	25.67	16.94
	North-Eastern	29.23	28.85	52.02	56.61
	Southern	24.19	22.31	5.59	5.71
	South-Eastern	20.05	15.75	16.72	20.74
	Total	100.00	100.00	100.00	100.00
Tamil	Coastal Northern	43.57	39.26	39.97	46.07
Nadu	Coastal	11.41	12.97	12.88	11.79
	Southern	33.87	30.89	29.73	31.89
	Inland	11.15	16.88	17.42	10.25
	Total	100.00	100.00	100.00	100.00

(Contd.)

Table 6.3 *(Contd.)*

0	1	2	3	4	5
Uttar	Himalayan	1.81	3.47	4.06	2.27
Pradesh	Western	16.69	22.29	39.92	39.14
	Central	23.63	19.65	21.00	23.52
	Eastern	46.96	47.10	24.10	21.67
	Southern	10.91	7.49	10.92	13.40
	Total	100.00	100.00	100.00	100.00
West	Himalayan	13.80	15.21	8.11	9.80
Bengal	Eastern Plains	38.23	34.23	17.43	19.04
	Central Plains	29.95	26.52	62.13	57.58
	Western Plains	18.02	24.04	12.33	13.58
	Total	100.00	100.00	100.00	100.00

The difference in CTP and share of poor is not wide in rural areas of Orissa and Madhya Pradesh, the two states with hard core rural poverty. Perhaps these two states are trapped in a low-level equilibrium and the poverty by itself is severe.

CTP and SP at Regional Level

Regional level CTP and SP given in Table 6.3 show the following.

I. CTP greater than SP:

(a) Rural: Northern Kerala, South Western Madhya Pradesh and Inland Central Maharashtra.

(b) Urban: Inland Northern Karnataka, South Western Madhya Pradesh, Inland Central and Inland Eastern Maharashtra and Coastal Northern Tamil Nadu.

II. CTP less than SP:

(a) Rural: Southern Kerala, Chhatisgarh region of Madhya Pradesh, Western Rajasthan, Western Uttar Pradesh and Western Plains of West Bengal.

(b) Urban: Southern Bihar, Eastern Gujarat, Inland Southern Karnataka, Coastal Maharashtra, Southern Orissa, Western Rajasthan and Inland Tamil Nadu.

The opposite movement of CTP and share of poor between the regions within a state is particularly evident in rural areas of (a) Northern and Southern Kerala and (b) South-Western and Chhatisgarh region of Madhya Pradesh, and in urban areas of (a) Eastern and Western Plains of Assam, (b) Inland Southern and Inland Northern region of Karnataka, (c) Coastal and Inland Central Maharashtra, (d) Western and North-Eastern Rajasthan and (e) Inland and Coastal Northern Tamil Nadu.

CTP and SP by Population Groups

The severity of poverty among occupation, socio-economic and religion groups is measured by Squared Poverty Gap (SPG). Treating each of these as sub-groups in the population, their Contribution to Total Poverty (CTP) is measured and compared with the Share of Poor (SP) computed from the poverty ratio. Similar exercises are made for gender groups and varying household sizes. These estimates are made in rural and urban areas at the national level.

Occupation Groups

Table-6.4 gives the poverty indices by occupation groups. The poverty ratio among the agricultural labourers is highest. They are also the group with high severity of poverty as their SPG (5.06) is nearly double the national rural average (2.77) and four times of that of the "others" (1.25).

The low-income low-inequality syndrome of the agricultural labourers culminating in high poverty ratio and severity of poverty is a part of the wider problem of unemployment and underemployment in rural areas. Besides, these can be traced to the pressure of population and the persistence of rigid social structure, largely based on caste. Independent enquiries also bring out the widespread underemployment and increase in population that has borne harshly on the agricultural labourers. In urban areas, the severity of poverty among the casual labourers is five times of that of the regular wage and salary earners.

The contribution of agricultural labourers to total rural poverty

Table 6.4 : Indices of Poverty by Occupation Groups

Occupation	Poverty Ratio (PR)	Squared Poverty Gap (SPG)	Share of Poor (SP)	Contribution to Total Poverty (CTP)
1	2	3	4	5
I Rural				
1. Self Employed in Non-Agriculture	32.21	2.08	11.24	9.77
2. Agricultural Labour	56.75	5.06	43.42	52.21
3. Other Labour	39.69	2.56	8.08	7.03
4. Self Employed in Agriculture	29.19	1.77	33.36	27.24
5. Others	17.57	1.25	3.90	3.75
6. All Population	37.23	2.77	100.00	100.00
II Urban				
1. Self Employed	36.19	2.93	43.17	40.58
2. Regular Wage & Salary Earner	20.93	1.36	27.47	20.72
3. Casual Labour	62.64	7.12	24.99	32.95
4. Others	26.48	3.00	4.37	5.75
5. All Population	32.28	2.81	100.00	100.00

(CTP) is 8.8% points higher than the share of poor computed from the poverty ratio whereas, the CTP of self-employed in agriculture is 6.2% points less. The CTP among the casual labourers is 8.0% points higher and that of regular wage and salary earners is 6.8% points lower than the share of poor. Thus, occupation specific anti-poverty programmes based on poverty ratio is at the disadvantage of agricultural labourers and casual labourers while unduly benefitting the self-employeds in agriculture and regular wage and salary earners.

Socio-Economic Groups

Table-6.5 gives the poverty indices for Scheduled Castes, Scheduled Tribes and "others" in rural and urban areas. In rural areas, the higher poverty ratio among the Scheduled Castes (48.3%) and Scheduled Tribes (52.0%) as compared to "others" (31.4%) is reflected in the SPG, which is nearly twice among the Scheduled Castes (4.01) and Scheduled Tribes (4.67) as compared to "others" (2.08). Thus, both the incidence and severity of poverty among the

Table 6.5 : Indices of Poverty by Socio Economic Groups

Socio Economic Group	Poverty Ratio (PR)	Squared Poverty Gap (SPG)	Share of Poor (SP)	Contribution to Total Poverty (CTP)
1	2	3	4	5
I Rural				
1. Scheduled Tribe	51.96	4.67	15.11	18.25
2. Scheduled Caste	48.32	4.01	27.41	30.54
3. Others	31.43	2.08	57.48	51.21
4. All Population	37.23	2.77	100.00	100.00
II Urban				
1. Scheduled Tribe	40.74	3.97	4.01	4.54
2. Scheduled Caste	49.84	5.14	21.16	25.36
3. Others	29.44	2.37	74.83	70.10
4. All Population	32.28	2.81	100.00	100.00

Scheduled Castes and Scheduled Tribes are more than the "others" The situation is by and large similar in urban areas. A comparison of the poverty indices among these three groups show:

(a) The poverty ratio among the Scheduled Castes is similar in rural and urban areas, but their severity of poverty is more in urban areas than in rural.
(b) The severity of poverty of the Scheduled Tribes in rural areas and Scheduled Castes in urban areas are indeed high.
(c) The Scheduled Tribes in urban areas though few in number are better-off than the Scheduled Castes.

Gender Groups

The poverty indices for male and female headed households are given in Table-6.6. The severity of poverty among the female headed households is marginally higher than male headed households. However, the closeness in the per capita consumption and inequality between male and female headed households point towards a decline in the historical economic inequality between men and women of almost a secular nature. The females in their entirety cease to be a deprived class, and if these are yardsticks, the issue of economic poverty does not require a view from the angle of gender.

Religion Groups

The poverty indices for six religion groups, viz., Hindu, Muslim, Christian, Sikh, Jain and Buddhist, at national level separately in rural and urban areas are given in Table-6.7. There is almost a one-to-one correspondence between the incidence and severity of poverty of the sub-groups formed on the basis of religious faiths. The share of poor and CTP are similar for the religion groups in both rural and urban areas.

The underlying phenomenon is that the poorest of the poor materially remain the same irrespective of their religious faiths. This is quite in contrast to the discrepancy between the share of

Table 6.6 : Indices of Poverty by Gender Groups

Household Types	Poverty Ratio (PR)	Squared Poverty Gap (SPG)	Share of Poor (SP)	Contribution to Total Poverty (CTP)
1	2	3	4	5
I. Rural				
1.Male Headed	37.37	2.76	93.50	92.74
2.Female Headed	35.46	2.95	6.50	7.26
3.All Population	37.23	2.77	100.00	100.00
II. Urban				
1.Male Headed	31.90	2.74	91.01	89.78
2.Female Headed	36.87	3.65	8.99	10.22
3.All Population	32.36	2.81	100.00	100.00

Table 6.7 : Indices of Poverty by Religion Groups

Religion	Poverty Ratio (PR)	Squared Poverty Gap (SPG)	Share of Poor (SP)	Contribution to Total Poverty (CTP)
1	2	3	4	5
I Rural				
1. Hindu	37.50	2.82	85.71	86.56
2. Muslim	41.27	2.75	10.97	9.83
3. Christian	30.25	2.51	1.69	1.89
4. Sikh	5.94	0.26	0.30	0.17
5. Jain	14.01	0.71	0.03	0.02
6. Buddhist	55.34	5.51	0.92	1.23
7. Others	35.79	2.07	0.38	0.30
8. All Population	37.23	2.77	100.00	100.00
II Urban				
1. Hindu	30.31	2.57	72.83	71.87
2. Muslim	49.23	4.43	23.14	24.22
3. Christian	21.34	1.82	1.70	1.68
4. Sikh	12.88	0.65	0.64	0.38
5. Jain	5.37	0.13	0.12	0.03
6. Buddhist	44.01	5.12	1.20	1.63
7. Others	31.71	1.73	0.37	0.23
8. All Population	32.28	2.81	100.00	100.00

poor and CTP by occupation groups. The difference between the share of poor and CTP for agricultural labourers and self-employed in agriculture in rural areas and for regular wage and salary earners and casual labourers in urban areas at the background of similarity between CTP and SP among the religion groups convincingly demonstrate that economics and not religion is the corner-stone of progress.

Household Size

Table-6.8 gives the poverty indices among the population of different household sizes. In both rural and urban areas, SPG is highest in six member households and least in two member households. The SPG

Table 6.8 : Indices of Poverty by Household Size

Household Size	Poverty Ratio (PR)	Squared Poverty Gap (SPG)	Share of Poor (SP)	Contribution to Total Poverty (CTP)
1	2	3	4	5
I Rural				
1.Single Member	16.87	1.57	0.51	0.64
2.Two Members	18.85	1.21	2.42	2.09
3.Three Members	23.90	1.54	5.78	5.03
4.Four Members	30.26	2.01	14.00	12.60
5.Five Members	36.31	2.60	21.14	20.43
6.Six and More Members	43.46	3.39	56.15	59.21
7.All Households	37.23	2.77	100.00	100.00
II Urban				
1.Single Member	11.40	2.48	1.10	2.76
2.Two Members	15.01	1.01	1.94	1.50
3.Three Members	16.31	1.03	4.80	3.52
4.Four Members	20.98	1.37	12.82	9.66
5.Five Members	28.79	2.35	20.87	19.69
6.Six and More Members	43.60	4.05	58.47	62.87
7.All Households	32.28	2.81	100.00	100.00

in single member household is greater than that of two member households. The reason behind higher severity of poverty among the single member households presumably lies in the deprived condition of widows, who under the confines of social norms, either prefer or are forced to live alone and suffer from endemic and quiet deprivation. There is a good deal of evidence on the deprived condition of widows in India, who represent about 8% of the female population. The mortality rates among elderly widows are higher than those among married women of the same age.

The poverty indices of the households of different sizes are based on per capita consumption, which is obtained by dividing the household's total consumption by its number of members. It is possible that there may be some relationship between household size and composition of the family such that adjustment with equivalence scale eliminates the link between poverty and household size. However, no attempt has been made here to apply equivalence scales to adjust for the differential needs of the family members.

There may also be the possibility of existence of economies of scale in consumption and the per capita cost of reaching a certain level of welfare may be lower in larger households than in smaller households. A sensitivity analysis of poverty ratio using alternative sets of equivalence scales and possible economies of scale parameters carried out in a study by Jean Dreze shows that larger households are more likely to be poor than smaller households when no adjustments are made. The households, which are typically small under conventional practice, are less likely to be poor than the average households. The experiments with a range of equivalence scales do not quantitatively alter the conclusions. However, the conclusions remain sensitive to even small adjustments for economies of scale in consumption.

The fact is that there is no consensus whether, or how much, to adjust consumption for economies of scale. In view of this, the poverty indices among the households of different sizes have been estimated here on the basis of simplest of all allocation rules, viz., to divide the total consumption of the household equally among all the members.

Poverty Indices: Relation with Consumption and Inequality

The way poverty is defined and measured in India makes the role of per capita consumption and inequality in consumption distribution important. The indices of poverty are negatively associated with per capita consumption and positively with inequality. This is evident from the correlation coefficients of the poverty indices with per capita consumption and inequality, given below.

Poverty Indices: Correlation with Consumption and Inequality

	Per Capita Consumption	Inequality
I. Rural		
(a) Very Poor	- 0.71	*
(b) Poverty Ratio	- 0.80	*
(c) Poverty Gap Ratio	- 0.75	*
(d) Squared Poverty Gap	- 0.68	*
II. Urban		
(a) Very Poor	- 0.65	0.30
(b) Poverty Ratio	- 0.71	0.22
(c) Poverty Gap Ratio	- 0.65	0.30
(d) Squared Poverty Gap	- 0.59	0.35

N.B. : * Indicate the correlation coefficients as not statistically significant.

The correlation coefficients reveal:

(a) The indices of poverty have a greater degree of association with per capita consumption than with inequality.

(b) The poverty indices in rural areas are more related to per capita consumption than inequality, whereas in urban areas these are more related to inequality.

The partial elasticities are estimated for each of the poverty indices with respect to per capita consumption and inequality from weighted log-log regression using the data of 59 NSS regions for which the poverty indices have been computed. In view of the varying size and population of the regions, the elasticities have been estimated from weighted regression using population proportions of the regions as weights. These are estimated for all the 59 regions and to trace the relationship especially for groups of regions, the partial elasticities are estimated for:

(a) Regions with per capita consumption less than the national average (i.e., rural regions with per capita consumption less than Rs. 281.40 per month and urban regions less than Rs. 458 per month).

(b) Regions with poverty ratio greater than the national average, (i.e., rural regions where the poverty ratio exceeds 37.2% and urban regions where the poverty ratio exceeds 32.3%).

Partial Elasticities of Poverty Indices

	Per Capita Consumption	Inequality	R-bar Square
I. All Regions			
I.Rural			
(a) Very Poor	- 3.28	1.09	0.63
(b) Poverty Ratio	- 2.22	0.31	0.64
(c) Poverty Gap Ratio	- 2.96	0.88	0.65
(d) Squared Poverty Gap	- 3.42	1.28	0.65
II.Urban			
(a) Very Poor	- 3.16	2.95	0.56
(b) Poverty Ratio	- 2.11	1.71	0.71
(c) Poverty Gap Ratio	- 2.93	2.74	0.66
(d) Squared Poverty Gap	- 3.34	3.50	0.68
II. Regions with Per Capita Consumption Below National Average			
I.Rural			
(a) Very Poor	- 4.05	1.08	0.55
(b) Poverty Ratio	- 2.16	0.08	0.47
(c) Poverty Gap Ratio	- 3.41	0.79	0.55
(d) Squared Poverty Gap	- 4.21	1.33	0.60
II.Urban			
(a) Very Poor	- 2.77	2.78	0.50
(b) Poverty Ratio	- 1.78	1.43	0.44
(c) Poverty Gap Ratio	- 2.69	2.65	0.51
(d) Squared Poverty Gap	- 3.16	3.52	0.54

	Per Capita Consumption	Inequality	R-bar Square
III. Regions with Poverty Ratio Greater Than National Average			
I.Rural			
(a) Very Poor	- 2.77	1.15	0.67
(b) Poverty Ratio	- 1.20	0.18	0.57
(c) Poverty Gap Ratio	- 2.29	0.86	0.66
(d) Squared Poverty Gap	- 3.06	1.40	0.70
II.Urban			
(a) Very Poor	- 1.83	2.47	0.61
(b) Poverty Ratio	- 1.05	1.18	0.48
(c) Poverty Gap Ratio	- 1.70	2.32	0.60
(d) Squared Poverty Gap	- 2.05	3.19	0.62

The sign of the partial elasticities underline the negative association of the poverty indices with per capita consumption and positive association with inequality. The partial elasticity of per capita consumption is maximum for SPG. The elasticities are greater for the regions with per capita consumption less than the national average than where the poverty ratio is greater than the national average. The partial elasticities of inequality confirm that relative inequalities are more pronounced in urban areas as compared to rural. The elasticity of Squared Poverty Gap and percentage of very poor is close.

7

THE ROBUSTNESS OF POVERTY ESTIMATES

There are considerable risks in accepting the poverty estimates made from the price updated poverty lines of a base year to mirror the extent of deprivation, particularly of food in view of the contrasts in the estimates of poverty from expenditure and calorie angle.

Poverty Estimates: An Assessment

The national poverty lines in the base year (1973-74) expressed as monthly per capita consumption expenditure of Rs. 49.09 in rural areas and Rs. 56.64 in urban areas correspond to a basket of goods and services, which satisfy the calorie norms of per capita daily requirement of 2400 kcal in rural areas and 2100 kcal in urban areas. These national level poverty lines in rural and urban areas are disaggregated into state-specific poverty lines using inter-state price differential, which in turn, are updated for subsequent years using a especially constructed state-specific price index considered to represent the cost of consumption basket of the poor. The state-wise poverty ratios are estimated from these state-specific poverty lines. The national poverty ratios are estimated as an average of state-wise poverty ratios. The national poverty ratio in 1993-94 is estimated as 36% with 37.3% in rural areas and 32.4% in urban areas. From these national rural and urban poverty ratios, the implicit national poverty lines are worked out as monthly per capita consumption expenditure of Rs. 205.84 in rural areas and Rs. 281.35 in urban. Ideally, these poverty lines should be able to meet the minimum calorie requirement. But the reality is different.

First, the NSS data on per capita consumption and calorie intake shows that the monetary expenditure required to satisfy the calorie norm in 1993-94 is Rs. 320 per capita per month in rural areas and Rs. 398 per capita per month in urban. These are 56% and 41% higher than the respective price updated rural and urban poverty lines. Secondly, 70% of the rural population and 56% of the urban population fail to attain the respective calorie norm (of 2400 kcal per capita per day in rural and 2100 kcal per capita per day in urban) in 1993-94. For the country as a whole, this is 66%, which is 30% point higher than the poverty ratio (of 36%) derived from the price-updated poverty line of the base year. This discrepancy (30% point) between the expenditure and calorie based poverty undoubtedly is a flack on the poverty estimates derived from price updated poverty line and calls for a thematic treatment of the measurement of poverty line and poverty.

Expenditure and Calorie Based Poverty:The Contrasts

All poor are not calorie deficient. Again, the calorie intake of all non-poor do not meet the norm, i.e, all calorie deficient people are not poor by the expenditure standard. These underline two separate phenomenon, (a) inadequacy of consumption expenditure to sustain a living, defined as poverty, and (b) inadequacy of calorie intake purported to be depicting undernutrition. The calorie intake and consumption expenditure in 1993-94 brings into surface the mix-up of poor and non-poor and the poverty estimates stands at this crossroads.

The price-updated poverty lines in 1993-94 are used to categorise people as very poor, moderately poor and lower and upper non-poor. By comparing the actual intake with the norm of 2700 kcal per consumer unit per diem (equivalent to 2200 kcal per capita per day) in both rural and urban areas, each group of population are classified into six levels of calorie intake, with three each from the angles of deficiency and excess of intake. These are:

(a) more than 30% calorie deficiency;
(b) 10% to 30% calorie deficiency;
(c) upto 10% calorie deficiency; and

Calorie intake exceeding,

(d) 10% of the requirement;
(e) 10% to 50% of the requirement;
(f) more than 50% of the requirement.

The matrix of calorie intake by aforementioned population groups is prepared for rural and urban areas at national level and also for major states. The national level estimates are given in Table-7.1.

Using the expenditure based poverty line, 37.3% of the rural population are classified as poor and the remaining 62.7% as non-poor. Using the calorie norm (of 2200 kcal per capita per day as mentioned above), 57.4% of the rural population are classified as calorie deficient and the remaining 42.6% attain the norm. From the expenditure-calorie matrix, it is observed that 6.1% of the rural population are poor but their calorie intake exceeds the requirement and 26.2% are non-poor but calorie deficient. Thus, the calorie intake of one out of every six poor persons exceeds the requirement and two out of every five non-poor remain calorie deficient.

In urban areas, 32.4% of the population are poor and the remaining 67.6% are non-poor. Using the calorie norm, 64.7% of the urban population are classified as calorie deficient and the remaining 35.3% attain the norm. From the expenditure-calorie matrix, among the urban population, 3.5% are poor but their calorie intake exceeds the requirement, and 35.8% are non-poor but calorie deficient. Thus, the calorie intake of one out of ten poor exceeds the requirement and more than half (53%) of all non-poor remain calorie deficient.

The Mix-up at State Level

The mix-up in the states is worked out in Table-7.2 for rural areas and Table-7.3 for urban. The state-wise percentage of calorie

Table 7.1 : Level of Calorie Intake by Population Groups

			Deficit			Surplus		Percentage
		+30%	10-30%	0-10%	0-10%	10-50%	50% +	of People
0	1	2	3	4	5	6	7	8
I. Rural								
1.	Very Poor	6.6	6.1	1.4	0.7	0.4	0.0	15.3
2.	Moderately Poor	3.8	9.3	4.0	2.6	2.3	0.1	22.0
3.	Poor	10.4	15.4	5.4	3.3	2.7	0.1	37.3
4.	Lower Non-Poor	2.3	9.6	6.6	5.7	9.0	0.9	34.1
5.	Upper Non-Poor	0.7	3.6	3.4	3.9	12.0	5.0	28.6
6.	Non-Poor	3.0	13.2	10.0	9.6	21.0	5.9	62.7
7.	All Population	13.4	28.6	15.4	12.9	23.6	6.0	100.0
II. Urban								
1.	Very Poor	7.3	5.5	1.2	0.5	0.4	0.0	14.9
2.	Moderately Poor	4.3	8.1	2.5	1.3	1.2	0.1	17.5
3.	Poor	11.6	13.6	3.7	1.8	1.6	0.1	32.4
4.	Lower Non-Poor	3.4	11.1	5.9	3.9	4.2	0.4	28.8
5.	Upper Non-Poor	1.5	7.6	6.4	6.3	13.5	3.5	38.8
6.	Non-Poor	4.8	18.7	12.3	10.2	17.7	3.9	67.6
7.	All Population	16.4	32.3	16.0	12.0	19.3	4.0	100.0

Table 7.2 : Mix-Up of Poor and Non-Poor in Rural Areas

S.No.	State	Poor		Non-Poor		Poverty Ratio (%)	Calorie Deficient Population (%)
		Calorie Deficient	Adequate Intake	Calorie Deficient	Adequate Intake		
0	1	2	3	4	5	6	7
1.	Andhra Pradesh	15.3	0.6	49.7	34.4	15.9	65.0
2.	Assam	42.2	2.9	31.9	23.0	45.1	74.1
3.	Bihar	46.3	11.9	12.6	29.2	58.2	58.9
4.	Gujarat	21.5	0.6	47.4	30.5	22.1	68.9
5.	Haryana	23.4	4.7	17.8	54.1	28.1	41.2
6.	Himachal Pradesh	24.8	5.6	18.9	50.7	30.4	43.7
7.	Karnataka	27.7	2.2	34.4	35.7	29.9	62.1
8.	Kerala	25.2	0.5	43.9	30.4	25.7	69.1
9.	Madhya Pradesh	34.3	6.4	22.2	37.1	40.7	56.5
10.	Maharashtra	34.9	3.0	37.2	24.9	37.9	72.1
11.	Orissa	38.2	11.5	13.5	36.8	49.7	51.7
12.	Punjab	11.4	0.6	31.9	56.1	12.0	43.3
13.	Rajasthan	20.2	6.3	16.3	57.2	26.5	36.5
14.	Tamil Nadu	31.4	1.1	42.4	25.1	32.5	73.8
15.	Uttar Pradesh	31.0	11.3	15.3	42.4	42.3	46.3
16.	West Bengal	32.9	7.9	21.5	37.7	40.8	54.4
17.	All India	31.2	6.1	26.2	36.5	37.3	57.4

Table 7.3 : Mix-Up of Poor and Non-Poor in Urban Areas

S.No.	State	Poor		Non-Poor		Poverty Ratio(%)	Calorie Deficient Population (%)
		Calorie Deficient	Adequate Intake	Calorie Deficient	Adequate Intake		
0	1	2	3	4	5	6	7
1.	Andhra Pradesh	35.7	2.7	35.1	26.5	38.4	70.8
2.	Assam	7.6	0.1	59.4	32.9	7.7	67.0
3.	Bihar	30.0	4.5	28.7	36.8	34.5	58.7
4.	Gujarat	26.7	1.2	40.0	32.1	27.9	66.7
5.	Haryana	15.3	1.1	45.4	38.2	16.4	60.7
6.	Himachal Pradesh	8.3	0.9	36.7	54.1	9.2	45.0
7.	Karnataka	36.8	3.4	29.1	30.7	40.2	65.9
8.	Kerala	23.5	1.0	46.9	28.6	24.5	70.4
9.	Madhya Pradesh	40.4	8.0	24.4	27.2	48.4	64.8
10.	Maharashtra	32.5	2.7	39.7	25.1	35.2	72.2
11.	Orissa	30.0	11.7	18.6	39.7	41.7	48.6
12.	Punjab	10.8	0.6	52.1	36.5	11.4	62.9
13.	Rajasthan	25.8	4.6	28.2	41.4	30.4	54.0
14.	Tamil Nadu	37.7	2.1	34.5	25.7	39.8	72.2
15.	Uttar Pradesh	29.6	5.8	31.3	33.3	35.4	60.9
16.	West Bengal	20.6	1.8	42.5	35.1	22.4	63.1
17.	All India	28.9	3.5	35.8	31.8	32.4	64.7

deficient persons is worked out by comparing the actual calorie intake in the states with the national level calorie norm. The percentage of rural population who are non-poor and calorie deficient:

(a) About 50% in Andhra Pradesh and Gujarat.
(b) 40 to 45% in Kerala and Tamil Nadu.
(c) 30 to 40% in Assam, Karnataka, Maharashtra and Punjab.
(d) About 20% in Madhya Pradesh and West Bengal.

In rural areas of Bihar, Orissa and Uttar Pradesh about 10% of the population are poor but not calorie deficient. Importantly, the calorie intake of 3 to 4% of the poor population in these three states exceed the minimum requirement by at least 50%. The lifestyle of these people, numbering about four million, may be worth exploring.

The percentage of urban population who are non-poor and yet calorie deficient:

(a) More than 50% in Assam and Punjab.
(b) 40 to 50% in Gujarat, Haryana, Kerala, Maharashtra and West Bengal.
(c) 30 to 40% in Andhra Pradesh, Himachal Pradesh, Karnataka, Tamil Nadu and Uttar Pradesh.

At least one-fifth of the poor in Madhya Pradesh, Orissa, and Uttar Pradesh are not calorie deficient.

Poverty Ratio and Calorie Deficient Population

The difference between poverty ratio and percentage of calorie deficient population is wide in the states with relatively low poverty ratio such as, Andhra Pradesh, Punjab, Gujarat and Kerala in rural areas and Assam, Punjab and Himachal Pradesh in urban areas. The two are close in poorer states such as, Bihar, Orissa and Uttar Pradesh.

The poverty ratio from the price updated poverty line does not correspond to the percentage of calorie deficient population and in the process, makes the estimate of poverty imprecise. The loss of precision arises as the price updated poverty line falls short of the consumption expenditure necessary to attain the calorie norm by a wide margin. The issue at stake is whether to use the price updated poverty line to calculate poverty ratio or poverty ratio be calculated from the poverty line derived from consumption basket of the latest year, which corresponds to the minimum calorie requirement.

The former produces a poverty estimate, which fails to capture the calorie deficiency of a fairly large number of people. The extent of deprivation, measured by the latter approach not only do not match other indicators of well-being but also underline immiserisation– a phenomenon, which is extremely difficult to endorse at the background of rising income and consumption in real terms. An alternative is to give a fresh look at the minimum requirement in view of the changing consumption pattern.

The precision of the estimates of poverty ratio depends on the extent of its match with the calorie norm. The pattern of calorie intake and poverty ratio together bring out the existence of poverty with excess of intake on one hand and calorie deficiency among non-poor on the other. This mix-up of poor and non-poor, viewed from consumption expenditure and calorie intake, places the estimates of poverty in a natural quandary and calls for a better understanding of the issues governing the definition and measurement of poverty.

The Issues

The state of poverty covers a wide range from debility due to malnutrition to falling short of having comfortable means. Traditionally, poverty has been defined in India in a manner, which is closer to the former. It is concerned with the minimum of provisions required to keep up health and working capacity in order to survive and maintain physical fitness and efficiency. This makes the concept of poverty absolute, and lack of a minimum requirement of food, clothing and shelter is termed as prevalence of poverty. It is on this basis that estimates of poverty are made in India.

The approach of poverty estimation has been to : (a) demarcate the entire country into two areas namely, rural and urban, (b) estimate separately their calorie norms from the respective age-sex-activity distribution of the population, (c) from NSS consumer expenditure data, estimate the monetary expenditure required to satisfy the calorie norms, which is known as the poverty line, (d) from the class-distribution of persons obtained from the NSS data on consumer expenditure, the number of persons below the poverty line are counted, (e) the number of persons below the poverty line as percentage to total population is termed as poverty ratio. The national consumption basket satisfying the calorie norm, separated by rural and urban areas is used uniformly for all the states, but its cost is estimated at the state's prices. It means that commodity composition of the basket remained invariant across the states and differs only to the extent of prices.

Poverty for any year can be worked out in an identical fashion, i.e., by estimating the calorie norm, its monetary expenditure equivalent, and the poverty ratio. However, stability of certain parameters and lack of availability of some data make it neither necessary nor permissible to do so. Due to stability in the age-sex-activity structure of the population, the calorie norm remains stable in the short or even in the medium term. The nominal value of the consumption expenditure required to attain the calorie norm (i.e., poverty line) may change due to change in the prices of goods constituting the consumption basket. The evaluation of the original (base-year) consumption basket at some later year's price is a daunting task as the prices faced by the poor are simply not available. Especially constructed state-specific price indices from the item-wise Consumer Price Index (CPI) of Agricultural Labourers in rural areas and CPI of Industrial Workers in urban areas are used.

The assumptions behind such updated poverty line are that these price indices represent the price rise of the consumption basket of the poor, and the consumption basket remains invariant over time. The consumption basket may change due to change in the relative prices as well as tastes and preferences. The choice thus gets restricted to either calculating the cost of the consumption basket (of the poor) for a later year in itself or deciding the consumption basket of the poor afresh and anew. But, the estimates of poverty based on the consumption basket of different years carry with it the loss of inter-temporal comparability. One of the main use of poverty estimates is to compare the levels of living over time. How good or bad the people are placed in different years with respect to a particular way of life? This moot question is sought to be answered by the poverty ratio and this is possible only when the ability or inability to procure a fixed consumption basket, either state-specific or at national level is used.

This estimate of poverty compares the availability or non-availability of the national consumption basket over a period of time at state level. The ability to acquire this consumption basket qualifies them to be termed as non-poor. More often the person is actually not consuming the same consumption basket, ostensibly due to the changing pattern of consumption. Herein comes the most crucial assumption in rationalising such a method of setting the minimum norm for a future year in the form of monetary expenditure. It is assumed that a person given the amount of money equivalent to poverty line will spend in such a way, in other words, will allocate his total consumption among different goods and services in such a manner that the individual is able to meet his calorie requirement. Such a proposition may fall apart under minimum provocation of non-availability or even inadequate availability of the desired bundle of commodities. The expectation that the same basket will be consumed by each and every person any time and anywhere within the state is indeed restrictive. As the poverty line is governed by fixity of the consumption basket, change of the basket overtime is likely to make the poverty calculations imperative. To cap it all, there remains the issue of exact calorie requirement of the individuals. How much calorie an individual really needs, itself is a matter of dispute. A form of gladiatorial sport by Prof. P. V. Sukhatme and V. M. Dandekar has produced an extensive literature centering around this seminal idea.

These estimates of poverty are known for exclusive reliance on private consumption expenditure of the households. The household expenditure arising from public consumption is not included in estimating this consumption. Critical is the exclusion of expenditure on the vast expanse of social services exerted through education, health, sanitation, water supply and housing, most of which provide basic necessities and help to bring about a measure of redistribution of income.

An exact definition of the minimum level of living and a precise estimate of the number of people failing to attain this minimum level has eluded the planners and the people. And, statistics about poverty depend on how poverty is defined. The methodological differences have allowed a bewildering array of numbers to gain currency, driving the common people to Hamletesque doubts. The estimation of poverty require a person to descent into the ravines of research for accurate information about the conditions of living of the people, their habit, quality of the consumption basket and its cost structure, running through the blizzards of facts and interpretation. Given the complexities of the problem and the data constraints, the estimates made here should be read keeping these issues in view.

EPILOGUE

Shortly after completion of the manuscript, the Key Results of Household Consumer Expenditure in India of the 55th Round covering the period July 1999 to June 2000 have been published by the National Sample Survey Organisation (NSSO). It is the first large sample survey of consumer expenditure of the NSSO conducted after the 50th Round (1993-94). The Planning Commission as the nodal agency in the Government of India for estimation of poverty in the country has released two sets of poverty ratios for the year 1999-2000 using the 7-day and 30-day recall data of the 55th Round. Thus, unlike in the earlier years, there are two sets of poverty estimates for the year 1999-2000. The poverty ratios estimated from the 30-day recall data and the 7-day recall data are given in Annexure-I and Annexure-II respectively.

The large sample surveys of consumer expenditure are important in the assessment of poverty and levels of living at state and sub-state level. But, the key results do not permit the kind of detailed exercises carried out with the 50th Round data. Nevertheless, certain broad magnitudes can be estimated using the techniques that have been described in the earlier chapters. In doing so, a number of sharp divergences can be discerned between the 55th and the 50th Rounds. The table below gives a comparative picture of some of the measures of distribution and poverty during these two rounds at the national level. The state-wise results are given in Annexure-III.

A comparison of the average and distributional parameters in 50th and 55th Rounds given below shows a phenomenal increase in the per capita consumption in both rural and urban areas and an impressive reduction in the inequality in its class distribution in rural areas. Between 1993-94 and 1999-2000, per capita consumption increased by 9.5% per year in rural areas and 11% per year in urban areas. Significant is the reduction in Lorenz ratio of consumption distribution in rural areas from 0.2816 in 1993-94 to 0.2595 in 1999-2000 at the background of a near stable value in the previous three decades. The increase in per capita consumption of poorer classes was also impressive. Per capita consumption of the bottom 30% of the population increased by about 11% per year in both rural and urban areas. The impact of rise in the per capita consumption and decline in the inequality is felt on the incidence of poverty. The rate of decline in the poverty ratio between 1993-94 and 1999-2000 is 5.1% per year in both rural and urban areas. In its impact, the number of non-poor during this period increased by 166 million as against increase in the population by 106 million. It effectively means decline in the number of poor by 60 million. Importantly, 85% of this decline occurred in the rural areas.

NSS 50th and 55th Rounds:A Comparative Picture

	NSS 50th Round (1993-94)	NSS 55th Round (1999-2000)
1. Per Capita Consumption (Rs per month)		
(a) Rural	281.4	486.0
(b) Urban	458.0	855.0
2a. Share of Consumption:Rural		
(a) Bottom 30%	15.9	16.8
(b) Middle 40%	34.1	34.9
(c) Top 30%	50.0	48.3
2b. Share of Consumption:Urban		
(a) Bottom 30%	13.6	13.4
(b) Middle 40%	31.7	31.7
(c) Top 30%	54.7	54.9
3. Lorenz Ratio		
(a) Rural	0.2816	0.2595
(b) Urban	0.3400	0.3417
4. Poverty Ratio		
(a) Rural	37.2	27.1
(b) Urban	32.3	23.6
(c) Total	36.0	26.1
5. Number of Poor (million)		
(a) Rural	244.0	193.2
(b) Urban	76.3	67.0
(c) Total	320.3	260.2

The substantial improvements, which can be observed in practically all the parameters in the 55th Round, however, need be treated with caution. The 55th Round consumer expenditure data is characterised by a significant departure in the survey methodology as compared to the earlier ones, particularly in respect of the choice of recall period. This requires a little bit of delving into the recall period used in the consumer expenditure survey of the NSS.

The choice of recall period in any survey always plays a critical role by influencing the level and accuracy of the estimate. NSSO's first experiment with recall period dates back to 1952-53, conducted in its 4th and 5th Rounds of survey on consumer expenditure. In order to ascertain the correct volume of consumption of food and a few other items, the consumption data in these two rounds were collected with week and month as reference periods from separate households. The consumption estimates obtained for week as reference period were higher than the figures obtained with month as reference period. However, the degree of difference between the two sets of estimates did not manifest consistency over the two rounds except for foodgrains (cereals plus cereals substitutes), where the week-based estimates were about 7% higher in rural areas and about 11-12% higher in urban areas, in both the rounds compared to month-based estimates. For food items taken together, the same differences were 10.4% and 22.3% in the 4th and 5th Round respectively in rural areas and about 14% in both the rounds in urban areas.

Around the same time, an experiment on the choice of recall period was conducted by P.C. Mahalanobis and S.B. Sen through a special study in March-April, 1952. The study was carried out in 1254 sample households spread over 76 villages in West Bengal and the experiments were conducted on clean rice, pulses, sugar and salt. The households were divided into four sub-samples. Consumption data on these items were collected from the first and the second sub-samples of households by interview method, using week and month as reference periods, respectively. For the remaining two sub-samples, particulars of consumption were obtained by actual weighing of these food items by the investigators. Here, the estimates of consumption obtained through interviews with month as reference period agreed fairly well with those based on weighing, while the figures based on week were appreciably higher. This finding established the choice and use of recall period to one month, which continued for the next four decades.

The issue of recall period again came under NSSO's experiment in its 51st Round (July 1994 to June 1995), which continued through the 52nd Round (July 1995 to June 1996), 53rd Round (January 1997 to December 1997) and 54th Round (January 1998 to June 1998). In each of these Rounds, the entire sample households were divided into two equal groups. In one group, the data, in conformity with the past practice, were collected with a uniform recall period of 30-days for all the items. For the other group of households, the recall period for different items were chosen as:

(a) 7-day for food, pan, tobacco and intoxicants,
(b) 30-day for fuel and light, miscellaneous goods and services and medical (non-institutional),
(c) 365-day for educational, medical (institutional), clothing, footwear and durable goods.

Thus, in this experiment the data on 30-day recall period and 7/30/365-day recall periods were collected from two different sets of households by two different investigators independent of each other.

The experiment with recall period was also extended to the large sample survey of the 55th Round *albeit* under an altered format. Instead of administering the 7-day and 30-day recall for food expenditure to the *different* groups of households as in the 51st to 54th Round, the NSSO in the 55th Round collected the consumption expenditure data from the households in the following manner:

(a) The data on consumption of food items (including pan, tobacco and intoxicants) were collected by using two different recall periods of 7-day and 30-day from the *same* households.
(b) The consumption expenditure data in respect of selected non-food items, such as clothing, footwear, medical (institutional) and durable goods were collected using 365-day recall period.

(c) In case of the remaining non-food items, the consumption expenditure data were collected using 30-day recall period.

Two different estimates of consumption were generated in the 55th Round. The 7-day recall data on food and 30/365 day recall data on non-food was termed as 7-day recall data, and the 30-day recall data on food and 30/365-day recall data on non-food was termed as 30-day recall data. Important to note that in this experiment the two sets of data were collected from the same households.

Consumption parameters, both average and distributional, estimated from these data collected independently from the two groups of households in the 51st to 54th Round and also from the same households in the 55th Round are given below.

Per Capita Consumption : 30-day and 7-day Recall
(Rs. per month)

Period/NSS Round	30-day Rural	30-day Urban	7-day Rural	7-day Urban
1. July 93 to June 94 (NSS 50th Round)				
a) Food	177.77	250.32	–	–
b) Non-Food	103.64	207.72	–	–
c) Total	281.40	458.04	–	–
2. July 94 to June 95 (NSS 51st Round)				
a) Food	188.89	271.49	245.69	365.67
b) Non-Food	120.54	236.58	108.08	235.82
c) Total	309.43	508.07	353.77	601.49
3. July 95 to June 96 (NSS 52nd Round)				
a) Food	207.75	299.98	274.20	399.53
b) Non-Food	136.53	299.28	130.47	278.72
c) Total	344.29	599.26	404.67	678.25
4. Jan. 97 to Dec. 97 (NSS 53rd Round)				
a) Food	231.99	320.26	295.64	424.46
b) Non-Food	163.02	325.19	149.64	311.61
c) Total	395.01	645.44	445.28	736.06
5. Jan 98 to June 98 (NSS 54th Round)				
a) Food	232.40	339.71	303.36	445.77
b) Non-Food	149.67	344.57	147.74	329.17
c) Total	382.07	684.27	451.11	774.94
6. July 99 to June 2000 (NSS 55th Round)				
a) Food	288.80	410.86	307.50	434.14
b) Non-Food	197.28	444.10	197.69	444.60
c) Total	486.07	854.96	505.20	878.74

Increase in Per Capita Consumption
(7-day over 30-day, Percent)

Period/NSS Round	Rural	Urban
1. July 1994 to June 1995 (NSS 51st Round)		
a) Food	30.1	34.7
b) Non-Food	- 10.3	- 0.3
c) Total	14.3	18.4
2. July 1995 to June 1996 (NSS 52nd Round)		
a) Food	32.0	33.2
b) Non-Food	- 4.4	- 6.9
c) Total	17.5	13.2
3. Jan. 1997 to Dec. 1997 (NSS 53rd Round)		
a) Food	27.4	32.5
b) Non-Food	- 8.2	- 4.2
c) Total	12.7	14.0
4. Jan 1998 to June 1998 (NSS 54th Round)		
a) Food	30.5	31.2
b) Non-Food	- 1.3	- 4.5
c) Total	18.1	13.3
5. July 1999 to June 2000 (NSS 55th Round)		
a) Food	6.5	5.7
b) Non-Food	0.2	0.1
c) Total	3.9	2.8

The above shows that in rural areas the food consumption expenditure collected from 7-day recall period in the 51st to 54th Round is 27 to 32% higher than that collected from 30-day recall period. Similarly, the total consumption expenditure derived from 7-day recall in the 51st to 54th Round is 13 to 18% higher than that obtained from the 30-day recall. Such differentials are more in urban areas. In contrast, the difference in per capita consumption between 7-day and 30-day recall data in the 55th Round is only 5 to 6% in case of food expenditure and 3 to 4% in case of total expenditure. The closeness in the per capita consumption obtained from the 7-day and 30-day recall data in the 55th Round at national level are also observed in the states.

The distributional parameters are measured by consumption

shares of bottom and top 30% of the population and as a measure of relative inequality by the Lorenz ratio of consumption distribution. The consumption shares of bottom and top 30% of the population and the Lorenz ratios are given below.

Pattern of Consumption Distribution:Rural

	30-day	30-day	30-day	7-day	7-day	7-day
NSS Round	Lorenz Ratio	Share of Bottom 30% (%)	Share of Top 30% (%)	Lorenz Ratio	Share of Bottom 30% (%)	Share of Top 30% (%)
1. NSS 50th	0.2816	15.94	49.95	–	–	–
2. NSS 51st	0.2960	15.78	51.01	0.2440	17.10	46.70
3. NSS 52nd	0.2762	16.21	49.71	0.2388	17.22	46.88
4. NSS 53rd	0.2900	15.36	50.98	0.2433	16.84	47.62
5. NSS 54th	0.2780	15.97	49.82	0.2379	17.13	47.25
6. NSS 55th	0.2595	16.75	48.33	0.2616	16.71	48.28

Pattern of Consumption Distribution:Urban

	30-day	30-day	30-day	7-day	7-day	7-day
NSS Round	Lorenz Ratio	Share of Bottom 30% (%)	Share of Top 30% (%)	Lorenz Ratio	Share of Bottom 30% (%)	Share of Top 30% (%)
1. NSS 50th	0.3400	13.55	54.66	–	–	–
2. NSS 51st	0.3667	12.81	56.82	0.3095	14.29	51.89
3. NSS 52nd	0.3583	12.98	56.51	0.3018	14.71	51.68
4. NSS 53rd	0.3500	12.98	55.50	0.3013	14.46	51.81
5. NSS 54th	0.3504	12.94	55.68	0.3133	14.07	53.97
6. NSS 55th	0.3417	13.41	54.74	0.3416	13.47	54.62

In the 51st to 54th Round, the consumption distributions in both rural and urban areas turn out to be more equal with 7-day recall data. The distribution pattern of the two data sets in the 55th Round, in direct contrast to the 51st to 54th Round, are almost identical. The near identical consumption distribution are also evidenced in the rural and urban areas of the states.

Using identical poverty lines for the 7-day and 30-day recall data, the poverty ratios computed from the consumption distribution of the NSS are given below.

Poverty Ratios : 30-day and 7-day Recall

NSS Round	Rural 30-day	Urban 30-day	Total 30-day	Rural 7-day	Urban 7-day	Total 7-day
1. NSS 50th	37.2	32.3	36.0	–	–	–
2. NSS 51st	41.2	35.5	39.7	22.8	18.3	21.6
3. NSS 52nd	37.6	29.7	35.5	19.1	15.2	18.0
4. NSS 53rd	35.9	32.3	34.9	20.7	17.8	19.9
5. NSS 54th	42.6	32.9	39.9	23.7	20.0	22.7
6. NSS 55th	27.1	23.6	26.1	24.0	21.6	23.3

As a result of higher per capita consumption and its more equal distribution, the poverty ratios in the 51st to 54th Round estimated from the 7-day recall data are about half of that estimated from the 30-day recall. In contrast, the poverty ratios estimated from the 7-day and 30-day recall data in the 55th Round are pretty close, not only at national level but at state level also.

What are the reasons behind such closeness in the 7-day and 30-day recall data in the 55th Round when such data reflect wide diversity in the 51st to 54th Round ? The main reason is that in the 51st to 54th Round, the two recall periods were administered to different households whereas in the 55th Round these were administered to the same households. In all probability, the collection of food expenditure data using two different recall periods from the same households in the 55th Round has not made the responses to the recall periods independent of each other and appears to have introduced an element of simultaneity into the data.

The closeness of the 7-day recall and 30-day recall data in the 55th Round clearly support such a hypothesis, though it is difficult to judge whether and to what extent the responses reflect the 7-day recall or the 30-day recall. The only thing that appears to be certain is that the comparability of the 55th Round data with the earlier Rounds stands compromised. To be specific, the 7-day recall data of the 55th Round are not comparable with the 7-day recall data of the 51st to 54th Round. Also, the 30-day recall data of the 55th Round are not comparable with the 30-day recall data of the earlier Rounds of the NSS.

In brief, the problem of the 55th Round is the possibility of simultaneity between the 7-day and 30-day recall period, which affects the comparability of this data set with the earlier ones. Nevertheless, the issue of whether 7-day or 30-day recall period is a better estimate of household consumption continues to be open. Doubtless, considerable research will have to be done in order to settle this issue decisively.

ANNEXURE - I

Number and Percentage of Population Below Poverty Line
by State - 1999-2000

(30-day recall period)

S.No.	States/U.T.'s	Rural		Urban		Combined	
		No. of Persons (Lakhs)	% of Persons	No. of Persons (Lakhs)	% of Persons	No. of Persons (Lakhs)	% of Persons
1.	Andhra Pradesh	58.13	11.05	60.88	26.63	119.01	15.77
2.	Arunachal Pradesh	3.80	40.04	0.18	7.47	3.98	33.47
3.	Assam	92.17	40.04	2.38	7.47	94.55	36.09
4.	Bihar	376.51	44.30	49.13	32.91	425.64	42.60
5.	Goa	0.11	1.35	0.59	7.52	0.70	4.40
6.	Gujarat	39.80	13.17	28.09	15.59	67.89	14.07
7.	Haryana	11.94	8.27	5.39	9.99	17.34	8.74
8.	Himachal Pradesh	4.84	7.94	0.29	4.63	5.12	7.63
9.	Jammu & Kashmir	2.97	3.97	0.49	1.98	3.46	3.48
10.	Karnataka	59.91	17.38	44.49	25.25	104.40	20.04
11.	Kerala	20.97	9.38	20.07	20.27	41.04	12.72
12.	Madhya Pradesh	217.32	37.06	81.22	38.44	298.54	37.43

(*Contd.*)

Table *(Contd.)*

13.	Maharashtra	125.12	23.72	102.87	26.81	227.99	25.02
14.	Manipur	6.53	40.04	0.66	7.47	7.19	28.54
15.	Meghalaya	7.89	40.04	0.34	7.47	8.23	33.87
16.	Mizoram	1.40	40.04	0.45	7.47	1.85	19.47
17.	Nagaland	5.21	40.04	0.28	7.47	5.49	32.67
18.	Orissa	143.69	48.01	25.40	42.83	169.09	47.15
19.	Punjab	10.20	6.35	4.29	5.75	14.49	6.16
20.	Rajasthan	55.06	13.74	26.78	19.85	81.83	15.28
21.	Sikkim	2.00	40.04	0.04	7.47	2.05	36.55
22.	Tamil Nadu	80.51	20.55	49.97	22.11	130.48	21.12
23.	Tripura	12.53	40.04	0.49	7.47	13.02	34.44
24.	Uttar Pradesh	412.01	31.22	117.88	30.89	529.89	31.15
25.	West Bengal	180.11	31.85	33.38	14.86	213.49	27.02
26.	A & N Island	0.58	20.55	0.24	22.11	0.82	20.99
27.	Chandigarh	0.06	5.75	0.45	5.75	0.51	5.75
28.	Dadra & Nagar Haveli	0.30	17.57	0.03	13.52	0.33	17.14
29.	Daman & Diu	0.01	1.35	0.05	7.52	0.06	4.44
30.	Delhi	0.07	0.40	11.42	9.42	11.49	8.23
31.	Lakshadweep	0.03	9.38	0.08	20.27	0.11	15.60
32.	Pondicherry	0.64	20.55	1.77	22.11	2.41	21.67
	All India	1932.43	27.09	670.07	23.62	2602.50	26.10

N.B.:

1. Poverty Ratio of Assam is used for Sikkim, Arunachal Pradesh, Meghalays, Mizoram, Manipur, Nagaland and Tripura.
2. Poverty Line of Maharashtra and expenditure distribution of Goa is used to estimate poverty ratio of Goa.
3. Poverty Line of Himachal Pradesh and expenditure distribution of Jammu & Kashmir is used to estimate poverty ratio of Jammu & Kashmir.
4. Poverty Ratio of Tamil Nadu is used for Pondicherry and A & N Island.
5. Urban Poverty Ratio of Punjab is used for both rural and urban poverty of Chandigarh.
6. Poverty Line of Maharashtra and expenditure distribution of Dadra & Nagar Haveli is used to estimate poverty ratio of Dadra & Nagar Haveli.
7. Poverty Ratio of Goa is used for Daman & Diu.
8. Poverty Ratio of Kerala is used for Lakshadweep.
9. Urban Poverty Ratio of Rajasthan may be treated as tentative.

ANNEXURE - II

Number and Percentage of Population Below Poverty Line
by State - 1999-2000

(7-day recall period)

S.No.	States/U.T.'s	Rural		Urban		Combined	
		No. of Persons (Lakhs)	% of Persons	No. of Persons (Lakhs)	% of Persons	No. of Persons (Lakhs)	% of Persons
1.	Andhra Pradesh	48.14	9.15	55.96	24.48	104.10	13.79
2.	Arunachal Pradesh	3.23	34.00	0.15	6.29	3.38	28.41
3.	Assam	78.27	34.00	2.00	6.29	80.27	30.64
4.	Bihar	322.96	38.00	43.64	29.23	366.60	36.69
5.	Goa	0.23	2.80	0.40	5.03	0.62	3.90
6.	Gujarat	36.87	12.20	24.80	13.76	61.66	12.78
7.	Haryana	11.13	7.71	4.33	8.02	15.46	7.79
8.	Himachal Pradesh	4.63	7.61	0.24	3.95	4.88	7.27
9.	Jammu & Kashmir	3.10	4.14	0.42	1.70	3.52	3.53
10.	Karnataka	47.02	13.64	39.35	22.33	86.36	16.58
11.	Kerala	18.20	8.14	17.73	17.91	35.93	11.14
12.	Madhya Pradesh	202.78	34.58	74.93	35.46	277.70	34.81
13.	Maharashtra	125.12	23.72	102.87	26.81	227.99	25.02

(*Contd.*)

Table *(Contd.)*

14.	Manipur	5.54	34.00	0.56	6.29	6.10	24.21
15.	Meghalaya	6.70	34.00	0.29	6.29	6.99	28.75
16.	Mizoram	1.19	34.00	0.38	6.29	1.57	16.50
17.	Nagaland	4.42	34.00	0.24	6.29	4.66	27.73
18.	Orissa	131.63	43.98	23.92	40.33	155.55	43.38
19.	Punjab	8.53	5.31	4.03	5.40	12.56	5.34
20.	Rajasthan	48.97	12.22	25.36	18.80	74.33	13.88
21.	Sikkim	1.70	34.00	0.04	6.29	1.74	31.03
22.	Tamil Nadu	73.19	18.68	45.81	20.27	119.00	19.26
23.	Tripura	10.64	34.00	0.41	6.29	11.05	29.24
24.	Uttar Pradesh	379.41	28.75	110.82	29.04	490.23	28.82
25.	West Bengal	154.04	27.24	31.06	13.83	185.10	23.43
26.	A & N Island	0.52	18.68	0.22	20.27	0.75	19.13
27.	Chandigarh	0.06	5.40	0.42	5.40	0.48	5.40
28.	Dadra & Nagar Haveli	0.26	15.31	0.02	10.89	0.28	14.84
29.	Daman & Diu	0.02	2.80	0.04	5.03	0.05	3.92
30.	Delhi	0.12	0.63	6.52	5.38	6.64	4.75
31.	Lakshadweep	0.02	8.14	0.07	17.91	0.10	13.72
32.	Pondicherry	0.58	18.68	1.62	20.27	2.20	19.83
	All India	1713.35	24.02	612.57	21.59	2325.92	23.33

N.B.: Notes are same as in Annexure-I

ANNEXURE - III
Average and Distribution Parameters in NSS 55th Round

S.No.	State	Difference in Per Capita Consumption 7-days over 30-days (%)		Lorenz Ratio			
				7 days		30 days	
		Rural	Urban	Rural	Urban	Rural	Urban
1.	Andhra Pradesh	5.3	2.5	0.2354	0.3087	0.2352	0.3128
2.	Assam	6.5	3.6	0.2082	0.3029	0.2011	0.3088
3.	Bihar	4.9	3.2	0.2090	0.3166	0.2059	0.3190
4.	Gujarat	2.7	1.7	0.2345	0.2846	0.2336	0.2865
5.	Haryana	2.0	2.5	0.2369	0.2909	0.2387	0.2864
6.	Himachal Pradesh	1.3	1.3	0.2318	0.2923	0.2350	0.2952
7.	Karnataka	6.6	3.1	0.2448	0.3181	0.2413	0.3227
8.	Kerala	2.7	2.1	0.2705	0.3190	0.2698	0.3214
9.	Madhya Pradesh	2.5	2.0	0.2406	0.3113	0.2419	0.3151
10.	Maharashtra	3.0	2.3	0.2571	0.3450	0.2582	0.3474
11.	Orissa	4.0	3.2	0.2466	0.2914	0.2434	0.2925
12.	Punjab	5.8	2.4	0.2526	0.2912	0.2384	0.2894
13.	Rajasthan	2.2	1.6	0.2088	0.2807	0.2092	0.2819
14.	Tamil Nadu	8.0	7.7	0.3051	0.4021	0.2791	0.3808
15.	Uttar Pradesh	2.1	1.7	0.2442	0.3289	0.2461	0.3297
16.	West Bengal	4.4	0.6	0.2206	0.3285	0.2237	0.3409
17.	All India	3.9	2.8	0.2616	0.3416	0.2595	0.3417

APPENDICES

APPENDIX-I

MATHEMATICAL SCAFFOLDING OF THE POVERTY INDICES

The incidence of poverty in India, as in most developing countries, is measured by poverty ratio. It is the percentage of poor in total population. The calculation of poverty ratio makes no distinction within the broad category of the poor depending upon their actual levels of income and deprivation. As a result, it fails to capture the depth and severity of poverty in an adequate manner. This has led the researchers to look for alternative indices to measure poverty and deprivation. And in fact, there are a number of them, of which three measures viz., poverty ratio, poverty gap ratio and squared poverty gap, have been worked out here. The evolution of these poverty indices and their mathematical scaffolding is given below for the sake of clarity.

Poverty Ratio

The Poverty Ratio (PR) in India is calculated from the percentage distribution of persons obtained from National Sample Survey data on consumption expenditure and an exogeneously determined poverty line depicting the money value of consumption requirements of food and non-food items considered to be the minimum requirement. The persons living below the poverty line are treated as poor. It is:

[1] $PR = q/n$

where q = number of persons with consumption expenditure less than the poverty line,

n = total number of persons.

The poverty ratio does not fully encapsulate the essence of poverty. In fact, it (the poverty ratio) has "little but its simplicity to recommend it".[1] Despite its weaknesses, Sen observed that the degree of support commanded by the poverty ratio is quite astonishing.[2] It is used to measure the incidence of poverty for it is simple to calculate and user-friendly. The bibliography of the poverty ratio in the Indian context is lengthy, to the surprise of one and all.

The intensity or depth of poverty of all the persons below the poverty line, i.e., of all the poor, may not and in reality is not the same. That all the poor are not equally poor gives rise to the question: how poor are the poor? The search for the answer begins here.

Consumption Gap

The consumption gap (CG) is the difference between the per capita consumption of the poor and the poverty line. It is a quantification of the amount of money needed by the poor to attain the poverty line level of consumption and used as a measure of the intensity of poverty. Aggregate consumption gap is:

$$[2] \qquad CG = \sum_{i=1}^{q} (x^* - x_i) \qquad \forall \; x_i < x^*$$

where, x_i = per capita consumption of each individual i, below the poverty line;
i = 1, 2, 3, ..., q
x^* = poverty line

CG is homogenous of degree one in consumption and poverty line and therefore expresses the gap in terms of money units. It changes when a person, due to change in consumption, either joins or leaves the poverty band. But it does not change when there is a

---

1. H. W. Watts, "An Economic Definition of Poverty", in *On Understanding Poverty*, (ed) by D. P. Moynihan, New York, Basic Books, 1968, Page - 326.
2. A. K. Sen, "Issues in the Measurement of Poverty," Scandinavian Journal of Economics, 81, 1979, quoted in A. B. Atkinson, "On the Measurement of Poverty", *Econometrica*, 55, July, 1987, Page-295.

transfer of income between the poor, making it insensitive to income transfer among the poor.

Normalised Poverty Gap

There are wide ranging ideas about the use of consumption gap to measure the intensity of poverty. The popular one is its normalised version, known as normalised poverty gap (NPG).

$$[3] \quad NPG = \sum_{i=1}^{q} (1 - x_i / x^*) \quad \forall x_i < x^*$$

NPG normalises the consumption gap in terms of the poverty line and hence is homogenous of degree zero in consumption and poverty line.

Income Gap Ratio

A combination of the features of NPG and CG produces an index which has been termed as Income Gap Ratio (IGR). It is:

$$[4] \quad IGR = 1 - xp/x^*$$

where xp = average income/consumption of the poor.
x^* = poverty line

IGR is the average shortfall of income of the poor from the poverty line. It has often been used as a measure of the depth of poverty. But, IGR is neither sensitive to income transfer among the poor nor to poverty ratio. It is homogenous of degree zero in income and poverty line.

IGR do not capture adequately the depth of poverty for in the event of a bunching of population around the poverty line, if persons close to the poverty line cross it then IGR can rise even as the poverty ratio falls.

Poverty Gap Ratio

Poverty Gap Ratio (PGR) is obtained by multiplying IGR by poverty ratio.[3] It is:

$$[5] \quad PGR = PR * (1 - xp/x^*) = PR * IGR$$

PGR adjusts the poverty ratio with the difference between the per capita consumption of the poor and the poverty line expressed as a percentage of the poverty line and adequately captures the depth of poverty. It is a measure of the magnitude of the effort required to shift the consumption of all persons below the poverty line to the level of the poverty line.

Sen's Index

The issue of intensity of poverty attracted the attention of Sen.[4] In his search for an answer to the question: "how poor the poor are", Sen developed an index of poverty by combining the features of: (a) incidence of poverty, measured by poverty ratio, (b) intensity of poverty, measured by income-gap ratio, and (c) inequality of consumption distribution of the poor, measured by Lorenz Ratio. This index is widely known as Sen's Index (SI) and can be expressed as:

$$[6] \quad SI = PR\,[IGR + (1 - IGR) * LRP]$$

PR = Poverty Ratio
IGR = Income Gap Ratio
LRP = Lorenz ratio of consumption distribution of the poor.

---

3. S. Clark, R. Hemming and D. Ulph, "On the Indices for the Measurement of Poverty", *Economic Journal*, 91, 1981, pp. 515-526, define it as Poverty Gap Ratio. The idea of multiplying IGR by Poverty Ratio (PR) originally came from Watts (1968), op. cit.
4. Amartya Sen, "Poverty: An Ordinal Approach to Measurement", *Econometrica*, 44, 1976, pp. 219-231; "Issues in the Measurement of Poverty", *Scandinavian Journal of Economics*, 81, 1979, pp. 285-307.

Sen's index is sensitive to the shortfall of income of the poor from the poverty line and also to the number of poor. Its value lies between zero and unity. It becomes zero when everyone's income exceeds the poverty line and unity when the income of everyone is zero. Thus, low value of Sen's index mean a low intensity of poverty; the intensity rises as the value of the index approaches from zero to unity. Sen formulated two axioms for a poverty measure to satisfy. These are:

(a) Monotonicity Axiom: According to this, given other things, a reduction in the income/consumption of a person below the poverty line must increase the poverty measure.

(b) Transfer Axiom: According to this, given other things, a pure transfer of income/consumption from a person below the poverty line to anyone who is less poor must increase the poverty measure.

Sen's Index and the variants developed around it though are decomposable, fail to satisfy the transfer axiom that increase in sub-group poverty must increase total poverty. Foster and Shorrocks have identified two specific sources on which the transfer axiom is violated. These are: (a) connection of Sen's Index with Gini measure of inequality (which is the LRP given in equation (6) above), for income distribution of the poor and (b) its reliance on rank order weighting.[5] This makes it not so well-suited for analysis of poverty by sub-groups.

Foster-Greer-Thorbecke Index

Foster, Greer and Thorbecke computed a poverty measure by combining (a) the poverty ratio, (b) the income distribution of the poor, measured by the coefficient of variation and (c) the intensity or depth of poverty, measured by Income Gap Ratio. This index is

---

5. James E. Foster and Anthony F. Shorrocks, "Sub-group Consistent Poverty Indices", *Econometrica*, 59, 1991, pp 687-709.

known as FGT index.[6] FGT is a family of index of which the Squared Poverty Gap (SPG) is the individual poverty gap raised to the power 2. This measure explicitly takes into account the higher intensity of efforts required to address the people who are progressively further below the poverty line in order to bring them out of poverty and thereby captures the severity of poverty among the poor.

The SPG is additively decomposable and also fulfills the two axioms (monotonicity and transfer axioms) proposed by Sen for a poverty measure to satisfy. Thus, in a sense it is an improvement over Sen's Index and the measures of poverty developed around it. The property of additive decomposability of SPG allows disaggregation of total poverty into poverty of sub-groups. Viewing the total poverty as a weighted average of sub-group poverty, it can quantify the effect of a change in sub-group poverty to total poverty or the sub-group contribution to total poverty.

The calculation of SPG runs as follows. The poverty ratio and consumption gap are worked out in the way described earlier. The inequality in the consumption distribution of the poor is measured by co-efficient of variation. Using these three, SPG is computed from the equation (9) given below. Equations (10) to (12) below show the decomposition. An interlude into the development of the index is made below.

The Derivation of SPG

The measure of poverty in FGT is defined as:

$$[7] \quad P_{\alpha}(x, x^*) = (1/n) \sum_{i=1}^{q} [(x^* - x_i)/x^*]^{\alpha}$$

where, $x = (x_1, x_2, \ldots\ldots\ldots\ldots, x_n)$
$=$ Vector of income/consumption in increasing order.

6. James Foster, Joel Greer and Erik Thorbecke, "A Class of Decomposable Poverty Measures", *Econometrica*, 52, 1984, pp. 761-766.

x^* = Exogenously set poverty line ($x^* > 0$)

$q = q(x, x^*)$ = Number of persons with income/consumption less than or equal to x^* i.e., number of poor.

n = $n(x)$ = Total number of persons.

$\alpha \geq 0$

The expression of FGT in (7) is a generalised version. The parameter α is interpreted as an indicator of "aversion to poverty". A larger α gives greater emphasis to the poorer of the poor. As α becomes larger, P_α considers only the position of the poorest of the poor. P_α is the mean over the whole population of a particular poverty measure which takes the value $(1 - x_i/x^*)$ for the poor and zero for the non-poor.

With α = 0 in (7),

$$P_o = q/n$$
$$= PR$$

Thus, with $\alpha = 0$, the equation in (7) gives Poverty Ratio.

With $\alpha = 1$ in (7),

$$P_1 = (1/n) \sum_{i=1}^{q} [(x^* - x_i)/x^*]$$

$$= (1/nx^*) \sum_{i=1}^{q} (x^* - x_i)$$

$$= (q/n)(1 - xp/x^*)$$
$$= PR * IGR$$
$$= PGR$$

Thus, with $\alpha = 1$, the equation in (7) gives Poverty Gap Ratio.

With $\alpha = 2$ the equation in (7) becomes Squared Poverty Gap (SPG). It is:

(8) $SPG = (1/n) \sum_{i=1}^{q} [(x^* - x_i)/x^*]^2$

$= (1/nx^{*2}) \sum_{i=1}^{q} [(x^* - xp) + (xp - x_i)]^2$

By rearranging,

$= (q/n)[(x^*-xp)/x^*]^2 + (q/n)^*(xp/x^*)^2 * [(1/q) \sum_{i=1}^{q} \{(xp-x_i)/xp\}^2]$

Here, q/n = Poverty ratio given in (1)
$(x^* - xp)/x^*$ = Income Gap Ratio.

$[(1/q) \sum_{i=1}^{q} \{(xp-x_i)/xp\}^2]$ = Variance of income distribution of the poor.

Using these, it can be shown that (8) is equivalent to:

(9) $SPG = PR^*[IGR^2 + (1 - IGR)^2 * CVP^2]$

where CVP = Co-efficient of variation of income distribution of the poor.

The expression in (8) is the mean of squared proportionate poverty gaps. The higher the value of α, the more sensitive the measure is to the well-being to the poorest person. As α approaches infinity, the measure collapses to unity, which only reflects the poorest person.

Decomposition of SPG

The decomposition of the generalised version of FGT given in (7) is carried out in the following way.

If the population is divided into m collections of households, j = 1, 2, 3, ..., m with ordered income vectors $x^{(j)}$ and population sizes nj then the generalised version of FGT index in (7) with $\alpha > 1$ or the version in (8) becomes additively decomposable with population shares as weights. This is given in (10).

$$(10)\quad P\alpha\,(x,x^*) = \sum_{j=1}^{m} (nj/n)\, P\alpha\,(x^{(j)}, x^*)$$

The decomposition in (10) allows a quantitative as well as qualitative assessment of the effect of changes in sub-group poverty on total poverty. Increased poverty in a sub-group will increase total poverty at a rate given by the population share nj/n. The quantity,

$$(11)\qquad Tj = (nj/n)\, P\alpha\,(x^{(j)}, x^*)$$

is the total contribution of a sub-group to overall poverty and

$$(12)\qquad CTPj = 100 * Tj / [P\alpha\,(x^{(j)}, x^*)]$$

is the percentage contribution of j-th sub-group in total poverty. This is termed as Contribution to Total Poverty (CTP).

APPENDIX-II

COMPOSITION OF NSS REGIONS

State	NSS Region	District
1. Andhra Pradesh	Coastal	Srikakulam, Krishna, Guntur, Nellore, Vizianagram, Vishakhapatnam, Prakasam, East Godavari, West Godavari
	Inland Northern	Mehaboobnagar, Adilabad, Medak, Rangareddy, Karimnagar, Hyderabad, Warangal, Khammam, Nizamabad, Nalgonda
	South Western	Ananthapur, Kurnool
	Inland Southern	Chittoor, Cuddapah
2. Assam	Plains Eastern	Bongaigaon, Sibsagar, Barpeta, Dibrugarh, Nalbari, Tinsukia, Sonitpur, Cachar, Lakhimpur, Marigaon
	Plains Western	Dhubri, Golaghat, Goalpara, Jorhat, Kamrup, Karimganj, Darrang, Hailakandi, Dhemaji, Nowgang
	Hills	Kokrajhar, Karbianglong, North Cachar
3. Bihar	Southern	Godda, Ranchi, Dumka, Sahibganj, Singhbhum (East), Deoghar, Gumla Singhbhum (West), Dhanbad, Giridih, Hazaribagh, Palamau, Lohardaga.
	Northern	Saran, Darbhanga, Sharsa, Madhubani, Gopalganj, Siwan, West Champaran, Madhepura, East Champaran, Purnia, Sitamarhi, Katihar, Araria, Muzaffarpur, Vaishali, Kishanganj, Samastipur
	Central	Patna, Begusarai, Gaya, Nalanda, Khagaria, Nawada, Bhojpur, Munger, Rohtas, Bhagalpur, Aurangabad, Jehanabad

State	NSS Region	District
4. Gujarat	Eastern	Sabar Kantha, Panch Mahals, Vadodara, Bharuch, Surat and Valsad (all partly) and the Dangs.
	Plains Northern	Sabar Kantha and Mahesana (partly) and Gandhinagar, Kheda, Ahmedabad.
	Plains Southern	Panch Mahals, Vadodara, Bharuch, Surat and Valsad (all partly)
	Dry Areas	Mahesana (partly) and Surendranagar, Kachchh, Bans Kantha.
	Saurashtra	Jamnagar, Rajkot, Bhavnagar, Amreli, Junagadh
5. Haryana	Eastern	Ambala, Yamuna Nagar, Kaithal,Karnal Kurukshetra, Panipat, Sonipat, Rohtak, Faridabad, Gurgaon
	Western	Jind, Mahendragarh, Bhiwani Sirsa, Rewari, Hisar
6. Karnataka	Coastal and Ghat	Dakshin Kannad, Uttar Kannad
	Inland Eastern	Chikmagalur, Kodagu, Hassan, Shimoga
	Inland Southern	Bangalore (urban), Mysore Bangalore (rural), Tumkur Mandhya, Kolar
	Inland Northern	Belgaum, Chitradurga, Bellary, Raichur Dharwad, Bidar, Gulbarga, Bijapur.
7. Kerala	Northern	Kasaragode, Malappuram, Wayanad, Kannur, Kozhikode, Palakkad
	Southern	Trichur, Alappuzha, Ernakulam, Pathanamthitta, Idukki, Kollam, Kottayam, Triruvananthapuram
8. Madhya Pradesh	Chattisgarh	Surguja, Durg, Bilaspur, Raipur, Raigarh, Bastar, Raj Nandgaon
	Vindhya	Tikamgarh, Rewa, Chhatarpur, Sidhi, Shahdol, Panna, Satna
	Central	Sagar, Bhopal, Damoh, Sehora, Vidisha, Raisen
	Malwa	Mandsaur, Jhabua, Ratlam, Dhar, Dewas, Ujjain, Indore, Shajapur, Rajgarh
	South	Jabalpur, Chhindwara, Narsimhapur, Seoni, Mandla, Balaghat
	South-Western	Khargone (West Nimar), Betul, Khandwa (East Nimar), Hoshangabad
	Northern	Morena, Datia, Bhind, Shivpuri, Guna, Gwalior.

State	NSS Region	District
9. Maharashtra	Coastal	Greater Bombay, Ratnagiri, Thane, Sindhudurg, Raigarh
	Inland Western	Ahmadnagar, Sangli, Pune, Sholapur, Satara, Kolhapur
	Inland Northern	Nashik, Jalgaon, Dhule
	Inland Central	Aurangabad, Osmanabad, Beed, Latur Parbhani, Jalna, Nanded
	Inland Eastern	Buldana, Yavatmal, Nagpur, Akola, Wardha, Amravati
	Eastern	Bhandara, Chandrapur, Gadchiroli
10.Orissa	Coastal	Baleshwar, Ganjam, Cuttack, Puri
	Southern	Phulbani, Kalahandi, Koraput
	Northern	Sambalpur, Mayurbhanj, Sundargarh, Dhenkanal, Keonjhar, Bolangir
11.Punjab	Northern	Gurdaspur, Kapurthala, Amritsar, Hoshiarpur, Ludhiana, Ropar, Jalandhar
	Southern	Firozpur, Bhatinda, Patiala, Faridkot, Sangrur
12. Rajasthan	Western	Ganganagar, Nagaur, Bikaner, Pali, Churu, Barmer, Jalor, Jaisalmer, Sirohi Jodhpur
	North-Eastern	Jhunjhunun, Sikar, Alwar, Ajmer, Jaipur, Bharatpur, Tonk, Sawai Madhopur, Bhilwara, Dholpur
	Southern	Udaipur, Banswara, Dungarpur
	South Eastern	Chittaurgarh, Kota, Bundi, Jhalawar
13. Tamil Nadu	Coastal Northern	Madras, Chengai Anna, Sambuvarayar, Thiruvannamalai, North Arcot (Ambedhkar) South Arcot
	Coastal	Tiruchirapalli, Thanjavur, Pudukkottai
	Southern	Madurai, Tirunelveli, Kamarajar, Ramanathapuram, Kottabomman, Kanyakumari, Dindigul-quaide Milleth (Anna) Pasupomthevar - Thirumaganar (Pasumpon-Mathamlingam), V.O. Chidambaram
	Inland	Dharampuri, Coimbatore, Salem, Periyar, Nilgiri

State	NSS Region	District
14.Uttar Pradesh	Himalayan	Uttarkashi, Garhwal, Chamoli, Pithoragarh, Tehri Garhwal, Almora, Dehradun, Nainital, Bareilly
	Western	Saharanpur, Muzaffarnagar, Bijnor, Meerut, Ghaziabad, Bulandshahr, Moradabad, Rampur, Badaun, Haridwar, Pilibhit, Shahjahanpur, Aligarh, Mathura, Agra, Etah, Mainpuri, Etawah, Firozabad, Sonbadra, Farrukhabad
	Central	Kanpur-Dehat, Kanpur Nagar, Fatehpur, Kheri, Sitapur, Hardoi, Unnao, Lucknow, Raibereli, Barabanki
	Eastern	Allahabad, Bahraich, Gonda, Faizabad, Sultanpur, Pratapgarh, Basti, Gorakhpur, Maunath-Bhanjan, Maharajganj, Sidhartha Nagar, Deoria, Azamgarh, Jaunpur, Ballia, Ghazipur, Varanasi, Mirzapur
	Southern	Jalaun, Hamirpur, Jhansi, Banda, Lalitpur
15. West Bengal	Himalayan	Coochbihar, Jalpaiguri, Darjeeling
	Eastern	West Dinajpur, Maldah, Murshidabad, Nadia, Birbhum
	Central Plains	24-paraganas (North), Calcutta, Howrah, Hooghly, Burdwan, 24-Parganas (South)
	Western Plains	Midnapur, Bankura, Purulia

APPENDIX-III

POPULATION BY NSS REGION

(Percentage)

States	Region	Region Share in the State Population		Rural-Urban Distribution	
		Rural	Urban	Rural	Urban
1	2	3	4	5	6
Andhra Pradesh	Coastal	44.08	40.85	74.57	25.43
	Inland Northern	37.46	44.01	69.82	30.18
	South Western	9.54	8.48	75.37	24.63
	Inland Southern	8.92	6.66	78.46	21.54
	Total	100.00	100.00	73.11	26.89
Assam	Plain Eastern	46.40	36.49	91.06	8.94
	Plain Western	46.28	57.25	86.62	13.38
	Hills	7.32	6.26	90.36	9.64
	Total	100.00	100.00	88.90	11.10
Bihar	Southern	22.93	40.88	78.75	21.25
	Northern	46.24	23.28	92.92	7.08
	Central	30.83	35.84	85.04	14.96
	Total	100.00	100.00	86.86	13.14
Gujarat	Eastern	20.70	18.28	68.27	31.73
	Plain Northern	24.03	35.69	56.13	43.87
	Plain Southern	15.73	12.10	71.17	28.83
	Dry Areas	16.08	8.18	78.88	21.12
	Saurashtra	23.46	25.75	63.38	36.62
	Total	100.00	100.00	65.51	34.49
Haryana	Eastern	59.44	72.31	71.55	28.45
	Western	40.56	27.69	81.76	18.24
	Total	100.00	100.00	75.37	24.63

(Contd.)

1	2	3	4	5	6
Karnataka	Coastal & Ghat	9.20	7.60	73.00	27.00
	Inland Eastern	12.73	7.40	79.36	20.64
	Inland Southern	29.82	47.30	58.48	41.52
	Inland Northern	48.25	37.70	74.09	25.91
	Total	100.00	100.00	69.08	30.92
Kerala	Northern	42.43	39.14	75.14	24.86
	Southern	57.57	60.86	72.51	27.49
	Total	100.00	100.00	73.61	26.39
Madhya Pradesh	Chattisgarh	28.62	19.98	82.60	17.40
	Vindhya	14.69	9.49	83.70	16.30
	Central	8.61	14.40	66.45	33.55
	Malwa	15.57	22.07	70.05	29.95
	South	13.09	8.25	84.01	15.99
	South Western	9.13	13.10	69.79	30.21
	Northern	10.29	12.71	72.86	27.14
	Total	100.00	100.00	76.82	23.18
Maharashtra	Coastal	11.42	45.35	28.53	71.47
	Inland Western	28.76	19.24	70.31	29.69
	Inland Northern	14.07	9.05	71.14	28.86
	Inland Central	20.66	9.17	78.12	21.88
	Inland Eastern	17.19	14.44	65.35	34.65
	Eastern	7.90	2.75	81.97	18.03
	Total	100.00	100.00	61.31	38.69
Orissa	Coastal	47.24	50.04	85.94	14.06
	Southern	18.17	11.63	91.01	8.99
	Northern	34.59	38.33	85.39	14.61
	Total	100.00	100.00	86.62	13.38
Punjab	Northern	55.60	63.95	67.45	32.55
	Southern	44.40	36.05	74.60	25.40
	Total	100.00	100.00	70.45	29.55
Rajasthan	Western	33.65	32.96	77.48	22.52
	North-Eastern	42.02	48.13	74.64	25.36
	Southern	12.59	6.43	86.85	13.15
	South-Eastern	11.74	12.48	76.04	23.96
	Total	100.00	100.00	77.12	22.88

(Contd.)

1	2	3	4	5	6
Tamil Nadu	Coastal Northern	28.67	41.41	57.16	42.84
	Coastal	20.84	12.22	76.69	23.31
	Southern	26.77	24.68	67.66	32.34
	Inland	23.72	21.69	67.83	32.17
	Total	100.00	100.00	65.85	34.15
Uttar Pradesh	Himalayan	5.87	8.03	74.71	25.29
	Western	31.85	44.43	74.33	25.67
	Central	16.55	20.78	76.28	23.72
	Eastern	40.98	21.56	88.48	11.52
	Southern	4.75	5.20	78.67	21.33
	Total	100.00	100.00	80.16	19.84
West Bengal	Himalayan	10.63	5.47	83.68	16.32
	Eastern Plains	29.80	11.76	87.00	13.00
	Central Plains	35.07	76.02	54.90	45.10
	Western Plains	24.50	6.75	90.54	9.46
	Total	100.00	100.00	72.52	27.48
	All India	–	–	74.96	25.04

INDEX